Bristol Railway Panorama

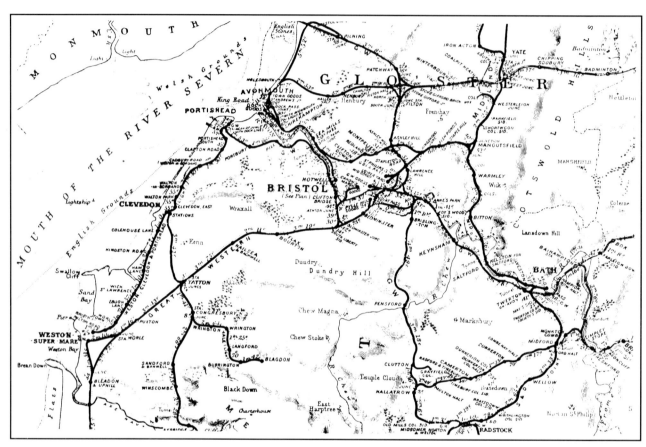

Extract from a Railway Clearing House map of 1918

Bristol Railway Panorama

Colin G Maggs

Millstream Books

First published 1990

Millstream Books
7 Orange Grove
Bath BA1 1LP

This book has been set in New Baskerville type by Ryburn Typesetting, Halifax
Printed in Great Britain by The Amadeus Press, Huddersfield

© Colin G. Maggs 1990

ISBN 0 948975 22 9

Contents

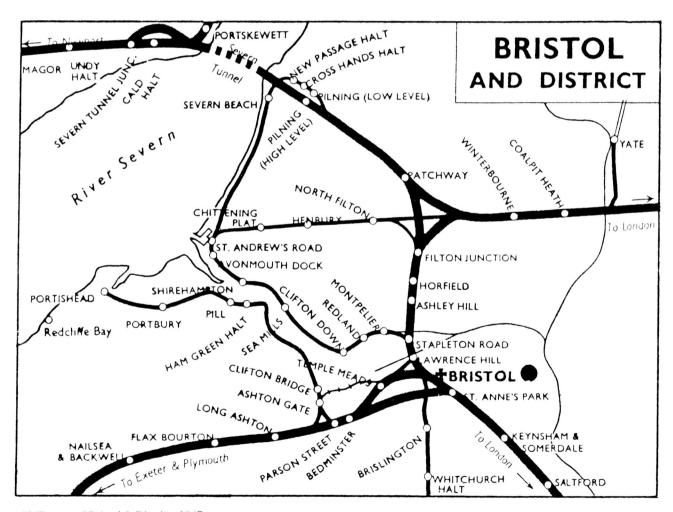

GWR map of Bristol & District, 1947

Introduction

Bristol is the centre of the area comprising Avon, Somerset, South Gloucestershire and West Wiltshire and, particularly in the days before the development of mechanical road transport, formed the hub of the area's railway network. To a large extent this is still true today, the main lines remaining though most of the branch lines have been closed.

This book is planned so that proceeding anti-clockwise it describes lines radiating from Bristol. An arbitrary start has to be made, so what better than to choose the Great Western Railway's Bristol to Bath line which celebrates the 150th anniversary of its opening in the year this book is written?

Colin G Maggs
Bath, April 1990

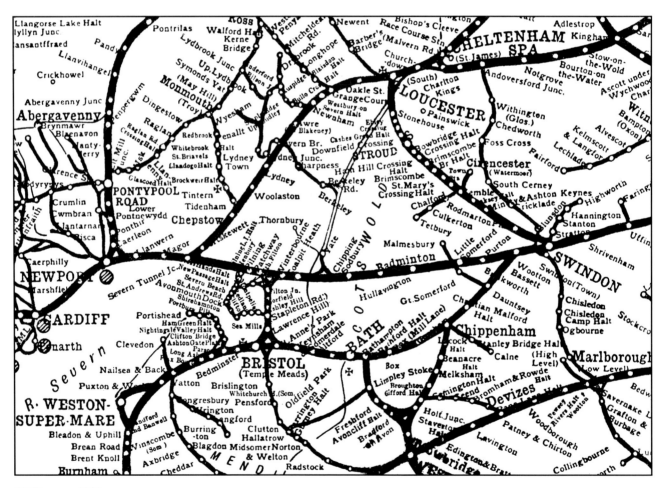

GWR map, c1930

1. Bristol to Bath

Early in the 19th century, Bristol was the second city in the kingdom, so with the development of the latest form of transport, the railway, it was not long before a link was projected with the capital. The first proposal put forward by Bristol merchants was the London & Bristol Rail-Road Company in 1824, with John Loudon McAdam, the great improver of roads, as its surveyor. He planned a turnpike road for riders and carriages to run alongside and in conjunction with the railway. This project was a little ahead of its time and proved abortive through lack of financial support as did some subsequent schemes, including one put forward by economy-minded landowners who suggested viaducts instead of embankments since these would have taken less ground space and provided shelter for cattle.

In the autumn of 1832, four Bristolians – George Jones, John Harford, Thomas Richard Guppy and William Tothill – formed a committee including representatives of the Society of Merchant Venturers and the Bristol & Gloucestershire Railway which had succeeded in running from Coalpit Heath to Mangotsfield, but had yet to enter the city. The meeting was held in Temple Back, the site later appropriately being covered by Temple Meads goods depot. The committee advertised for an engineer and had the daring foresight to appoint the 26-year old Isambard Kingdom Brunel on 7th March 1833. Brunel prepared a report which was considered at a public meeting in the Guildhall, Bristol on 30th July when a resolution was passed to form a company which became the Great Western Railway.

As with motorway construction today, the work was too great to be done as an entity, but was planned to be opened in sections. The prospectus asked for a capital of £3m and announced that the first lengths opened would be from London to Reading, and Bristol to Bath. It went on to observe that goods took a day to travel from Bristol to Bath by river, but on the new railway would take only 25 minutes. Between Bristol and Bath the line was carefully planned to be virtually flat. The promoters had the choice of either skirting Bath at a distance of 1½ miles and communicating by a branch, or passing through without injuring its attractiveness. The first option involved a junction with the Bristol & Gloucestershire Railway, then a tunnel through Freezing Hill, followed by a descent of the Swainswick Valley to Lambridge, but the latter option was chosen. A serious plan for lighting the railway by gas throughout from Bristol to London was not adopted.

The promoters certainly found a demand for a railway. Francis Berry, a linen draper of Bath, declared that there was a depreciation of 20 per cent in goods owing to the change of fashion while they were in course of transit by barge! A Bristol wine merchant complained that beer and spirits conveyed by canal were frequently pilfered or adulterated en route, a favourite practice being the unlawful abstraction of a portion of the contents of a vessel and refilling the space with water – a process known as 'sucking the monkey'.

Water Carriage.

The Kennet and Avon Canal affords a direct Communication with London; and Goods are in general conveyed thither in five or six days from the following Warehouses:

A. J. DREWE's (late Betts and Drewe) Fly-Boats, daily, to and from Steel-yard Wharf, Thames street, London; and Darlington Wharf, near Sydney wharf, Bath, in five days regularly.

EUCLID SHAW and Co.'s Fly Boats, from Bull Wharf, Upper Thames street, London; to Sydney Wharf, Bath, in five days; and Bull Wharf, Redcliffe street, Bristol, in six days.

C. and R. PARKER'sFly-Boats, to and from Redcliff Back, Bristol, and Dorchester street, Bath, every day; and deliver goods at each place every morning; and to Marlborough, Bradford, Trowbridge, Devizes, Salisbury, Andover, &c., three times a week.

The *City of Bath*, Steam-Boat, for the conveyance of Passengers and Goods to and from Bristol; leaves the Old Bridge, Bath, every morning, (except Sunday) at 8, and returns the same evening.

Pre-railway era: details of steam and fly boats between Bath and Bristol. *Bath Directory, 1833*

CLIFTON a four inside Coach, every morning, (except Sunday) at 10.

——— A four-inside Coach, every afternoon, (except Sunday) at 3 and 4.

BRISTOL Coaches every morning at 7 and 8; ditto at 10, 11, and 12 (except Sunday); every afternoon at 1; ditto at 2, 3, (except Sunday) 4, and half-past 4; ditto 5 and at 6; ditto at 7 (except Sunday); ditto every evening at 8.

FROME every morning at half-past 8, and every evening (except Sunday) at a quarter past 6 o'clock.

SALISBURY, every morning, (except Sunday) at 8 and half-past 8.

WESTON-SUPER-MARE, every morning at 7 during the Summer season.

Performed by M. PICKWICK, & Co.

Passengers and Parcels forwarded, with the greatest dispatch, from this Office, to all parts of the Kingdom.

Black Carriages and Horses for Funerals.

Pre-railway era: Coaches to Bristol from the White Hart Inn, Bath. *Bath Directory, 1833*

Great Western Railway Office.

23rd October, 1833.

Considerable progress has been made in the establishment of this Company, and in the preliminary arrangements for the Railway, since the accompanying prospectus was issued to the public in the month of August last.

The line of road has in the interval been accurately surveyed and selected by the Directors, and the result of the survey is in every respect satisfactory.

The distance between London and Bristol will be reduced to 117 miles.

The calculation of revenue has been confirmed by minute enquiries, and may be safely relied upon.

Under these circumstances, the Directors of the Great Western Railway Company have resolved to make application, in the approaching Session, for authority to construct the Sections of the main Railway extending between London and Reading, (with a Branch to Windsor) and between Bristol and Bath, thereby rendering the ultimate completion of the whole line more certain, upon a further application to Parliament in the following year.

This measure is sanctioned by the provisions of the Parliamentary Contract, and is recommended by many essential advantages to the Proprietors.

The standing Orders of the two Houses of Parliament, referable to this partial line of Railway, will be complied with by a deposit of the Plans and Book of reference, previously to 30th November.

The number of Shares required for this part of the undertaking will be 12,500, of which 2,500 will be reserved for the proprietors of land, &c. and consequently no application for shares can be entertained so soon as 10,000 shall have been subscribed; of which a very considerable proportion has been already allotted.

The estimates of cost and revenue for the sections of the line adverted to, are highly satisfactory; and this course of proceeding promises a beneficial and quicker return to the Proprietors for the capital invested.

It is intended also by the Directors, to insure to the Proprietors a preferable option of taking an equal number of new Shares upon the future extension of the subscription list to complete the line between Reading and Bath; thereby reserving to the original subscribers whatever advantage may accrue from any improved value in the Shares.

Subscribers will not be answerable beyond the amount of their respective Shares.

The Parliamentary Notices will be given in the first week in November.

Application for the Shares remaining to be allotted to complete the limited subscription list, should be immediately addressed to the Secretary in London or Bristol, from whom the Prospectus may be obtained.

GWR Prospectus, 1833

The necessary Parliamentary powers were granted by an Act which received Royal Assent on 31st August 1835. The GWR Bill was an enormous document 250 feet in length, weighed over nine pounds and was made up of 130 skins or pieces of parchment each about 23 inches long and 10 inches wide. Two months after the Act was passed, the far-reaching and costly decision was made to build the line to the broad gauge of 7 ft 0¼ inch instead of 4 ft 8½ inches – but more of this later.

No time was wasted and the first stage of the work began in September, while during the autumn and winter most of the land was purchased. In March 1836, William Ranger signed a major contract for constructing a length from Avon Bridge, Bristol to a field in the parish of Keynsham, this contract including the three tunnels at Brislington. He, too, wasted no time and started work in April, and a year later the heavy embankment west of Keynsham, much of Bristol No 3 Tunnel and the Avon Bridge were finished. It was hoped that the line would be opened during the spring of 1838, but Ranger fell into financial difficulties. His contract stated that if his work was unsatisfactory the GWR could seize his plant and complete the work itself. After giving notice, this it did in the spring of 1838. Ranger valued his plant at £70,000. He took legal proceedings and engaged in a long and expensive lawsuit which was not settled until it reached the House of Lords in 1855. The GWR sublet the three Bristol tunnels in small lengths and gave the remainder of Ranger's contract to David McKintosh.

A variety of other contractors was used over the 11¾-mile stretch: Messrs Brown & Son being responsible for the passenger station at Temple Meads; Thomas Wilcox & Sons for Temple Meads goods station; James Ridewood for the viaduct approaching Bath station; James Scott for the station itself; and William Chadwick for the bridge over the Avon immediately west of Bath station. It was reported in August 1838 that 600 men were engaged at Saltford on the tunnel and other works. By August 1839 most of the civil engineering was complete except for the bridge over the Floating Harbour at Bristol where difficulties were experienced with the foundations due to Ranger's bad workmanship. At Bath, erecting the bridge and station had not even begun. The spring of 1840 was foreseen as the opening date, but then a wet winter caused delays, the Avon bursting its banks, flooding the station site and preventing bridge work being carried out. This weather caused a delay of four months.

The Directors announced that the line to Bath would open on the last day of August. Six of Daniel Gooch's new engines had arrived and were ready. *Arrow* and *Dart* had been built by Stothert, Slaughter & Co at Bristol, while *Fire Ball, Spit Fire, Lynx* and *Meridian* came from various makers in the north of England. *Fire Ball* and *Meridian* arrived in parts by barge and were assembled in Saltford Tunnel.

A copper plate photographed in Twerton Tunnel, c1903. 'July 1840' probably marks the completion of the tunnel.

Author's Collection

A contemporary Bristol newspaper gave an account of the initial trip between Bristol and Bath:

The first railway journey between the cities of Bristol and Bath was made on Friday last the 21st August, 1840, and in case this notice of it should go down to future times, when perhaps still speedier means of locomotion may be in fashion we think it worth while to give some particulars of the trip. The party consisted of five of the Directors: Messrs R Bright, W Tothill, T R Guppy, C B Fripp and R Scott, attended by Mr Brunel, Mr Clarke, the Superintendent and some other officers of the Company. In consequence of the rails not being quite finished at the station in Temple Meads, it was not easy to get a carriage upon the line at the Engine-house, and the party were therefore content 'to take their places' on the engine and tender. The engine selected for the first part of the journey was the 'Arrow', the first Bristol made locomotive and a very creditable specimen it is of the skill of the manufacturers, Messrs Stothert & Co, of this City.

The start was made from a point nearly opposite to the engine-house at 20 minutes after 4 o'clock, and after threading the darksome passage of Tunnels Nos 1, 2 and 3, and skimming over the new embankment at Fox's Wood, the engine was stopped at the Keynsham Station at 4h. 30m. Here the Directors alighted and after a delay of 8 minutes they started again, on the other line of rails, with the 'Meridian', a fine engine from the manufactory of Messrs Hawthorn & Co, of Newcastle. As the engine flew onwards, the party was greeted with hearty cheers from bands of workmen and spectators at different points, and after making a short stoppage near the Cross Posts Bridge [about ½ mile west of Twerton Tunnel], to take up the assistant engineer, Mr Frere (who we regret to hear has lately met with a serious accident from a fall), the Directors completed their trip to Bath, arriving at the Oak Street Viaduct at 4h. 53m.

After staying some time to inspect the bridge over the Avon the party again took their places on the engine and the start was made at 32 minutes after 5. A short stoppage was again made at the Cross Posts Bridge and then the Keynsham Station was reached at 5h

45m. Here the Directors again 'took flight' by the 'Arrow', which landed them safely at the engine-house in St Philip's in 10½ minutes. In consequence of the numerous workmen still at work on the line it was not thought prudent to make any trial of speed, but our readers will see that the trip was performed to Bath in 33 minutes including two stoppages, one of these 8 minutes. Such a run as this must be quite sufficient to secure an abundant traffic as soon as the line is opened to the public.

A great effort was made to open the railway on time and during the week before 31st August, a thousand men were working on and near the river bridge west of Bath station. They carried on the task all night aided by light from huge fires. On 31st August there was no special opening ceremony, but flags were hoisted to mark the occasion. *Meridian*, whose driver was Cuthbert Davison recently arrived from Newcastle-upon-Tyne where he had gained experience of locomotive driving, was to have hauled the first train, but *Fire Ball* was ready earlier and the honour fell to her. Davison took the next train and later said that he never forgot the thousands of enthusiastic people he saw along the route and the immense crowds gathered at Bath.

A few minutes before 8.00am on 31st August a train of three first class and five second class coaches was nearly filled. The bell was rung and *Fire Ball*, gaily decorated with flags, left just after 8 o'clock, less than half an hour after the last rail into the station had been laid. All along the route crowds lined the railway. After threading Bristol Tunnels Nos 1 and 2 'in the twinkling of an eye', as one reporter put it, 'the passengers being frightened by the noise and prolonged darkness of Tunnel No 3, relieved only by the glimmer of railway policemen's torches in recesses', the train arrived at Keynsham, the only intermediate station. Here it stopped for three minutes. Bath was reached in 33 minutes from Bristol. It was greeted by the station staff in their green uniforms, and the Directors went to the White Lion in High Street for a 'splendid breakfast'. Peals from the Abbey bells and occasional discharges from guns marked the day as one of special rejoicing.

The first train from Bath, drawn by *Arrow*, left late due to a defective wheel on a second class coach. Delayed more than half an hour, the second train from Bristol arrived first but with

An early engraving by J Hollway, 10 Union Street, Bath, of a train crossing the timber bridge over the Avon immediately west of Bath station. Further downstream is the Old Bridge. The tow-path, horse-drawn barges and horse can be seen on the left.

Author's Collection

fewer passengers than the first, 'possibly', said a reporter, 'because nervous Bristolians wanted to make sure their friends were safe before making the journey'. After the train had started, the alarm was given that one of the carriages was on fire and a further delay was caused by a stop at Twerton for examination. It was found that a wheel grating on the under part of the carriage was causing sparks. It must have been a design fault as this happened on several trains during the day. Throughout 31st August people crowded into the coaches for the novelty of the ride 'with none of the bumpiness of some other lines'.

Trains took 25 minutes from Bath to Bristol, including the stop at Keynsham. Some 5,880 passengers were carried on the first day in ten trains each way and £476 was received in fares compared with the £226 taken on the opening of the line between Paddington and Maidenhead. Receipts at Bath were £231, at Bristol £224 and at Keynsham £21. The first class single fare was 2s 6d. The original timetable continued until December when stations were opened at Saltford and Twerton and an extra train added each way.

Moses Pickwick, a Bath coach operator, capitalised on the opening of the railway and organised a horse bus service at sixpence a journey to meet every train, the round trip starting and ending at his White Hart Inn. Pickwick ran coaches on behalf of the railway between Bath and the London end of the line until rail communication was completed throughout in 1841. It has been said that Dickens, who at one time lived in Bath, took his name for the character in *Pickwick Papers*. Buses and coaches also went to and from the station at Temple Meads.

To meet railway competition, a half-hourly service of coaches was put on the road between Bath and Bristol. As many as 70 coaches had run daily between the two cities, but the opening of the railway reduced the number to 11 or 12. One coach continued to carry passengers at one penny a mile from Bristol to London until October 1843.

The *Bristol Standard* claimed that *Arrow* was the fastest locomotive on the line and ran between Bath and Bristol in 13 minutes, reaching a speed of 100 mph. Fast it might have been, but this certainly strains credibility.

In its opening week the railway played a part in the arrest of a criminal. A gentleman from Bath arriving at Bristol found that he had been robbed of £120. He suspected a man who had boarded the Bath train, which by then had left. The robber's victim was strapped for safety to an engine which carried him to Bath on the Down line in 11½ minutes and overtook the train on which the thief was travelling, this correctly using the Up line. Immediately the special arrived at Bath the railway police were informed and the thief arrested as he stepped off the train.

It took passengers some time to adapt to the company's rules. No smoking was permitted on GWR premises and a Directors' minute dated 14th October 1840 read:

> The circumstances attending the case of two first class passengers having on the 9th instant smoked cigars at the Bath station, where they were remonstrated with by the police sergeant, who showed them the Bye-laws of the Company, and one of whom afterwards resumed smoking in the carriage between Bath and Keynsham, was reported to the Committee, by the Secretary, who had been directed to take steps for the infliction of the penalty, having presented a letter from the offending parties strongly expressive of their contrition, it was ordered that further proceeding should be stayed on their paying the amount of the fine incurred – Forty shillings – to be appropriated in donations of £1 each, to the Bristol Infirmary and to the General Hospital, with an announcement of the same to the public in each of the Bristol newspapers.

Third class traffic and goods were not carried between Bristol and Bath until the opening of the line from London on 30th June 1841 when a beflagged train carrying the Directors left Paddington at 8.00am, arriving at Bristol at noon. The GWR was most class-conscious and at principal stations, second class passengers were not permitted to come into contact with those travelling first. In June 1842 there were pens for first and second class passengers on the Up platform at Bath and first class passengers could use a waiting room adjoining their pen. Even first and second class exits from the platforms were provided. First class passengers had the luxury of enclosed carriages, while those of the second class were open to the weather. Third class passengers were treated like cattle and carried only by goods train.

In 1841 Sir Frederick Smith reported to the Board of Trade:

> The third class carriages have seats 18 inches high, but the sides and ends are only two feet above the floor, so that a person standing up, either when the train is unexpectedly put in motion or stopped, is, if near the side or end, in great danger of being thrown out of the carriage, and those sitting near the sides are also in danger of falling; besides which, the exposure to the cutting winds of the winter must be very injurious to the traveller, who, if proceeding from London to Bristol, often remains exposed for ten or twelve hours a great part of which is in the night-time.

The danger of being exposed to the weather was all too true. On Friday 14th March 1845, John Jonathan, about 50 years of age, travelled to Bath by the 10.10am third class train from Bristol. On arrival, Porter John Fennell found that Jonathan was unable to leave his coach and so assisted him to the platform where he expressed a wish for a pint of ale. After the train had left, Fennell carried him down the stairs and asked Charles Todd, one of the urchins who infested the station, to take him to William Knee's *Railway Station Tavern* at 6 Newark Street. Before crossing Dorchester Street John Jonathan collapsed and so was conveyed to Bright's the chemist, 24/25 Southgate Street, and medical aid sought from Doctor John Lloyd of 31 Claverton Street. It was of no avail and he died.

At the inquest held the following day in the *Full Moon*, Southgate Street, the jury viewed the very emaciated body. John Jonathan's widow said that her husband, a wire worker, had been ill for 15 years and had had a severe cough on 1st March. As there was not enough money for them both to travel by train, she saw him off at Bristol and then walked to Bath, arriving about 3.00pm to find him dead. To help protect him from the elements he had taken the precaution of wearing two pairs of

GWR timetable from Paddington to Bridgewater from *Bradshaw's Railway Companion*, 1842.

The interior of Brunel's train shed at Bristol. Left is the arrival platform; notice the pillars placed awkwardly near its edge. Centre: the roads for spare rolling stock; notice men hand-shunting a wagon carrying a brougham. Right is the departure platform with a train about to leave.

Engraving by J C Bourne, c1845

trousers, two waistcoats, two body coats and a warm woollen scarf round his neck.

The jury brought in a verdict 'That the deceased died by the visitation of God, but that his death was accelerated by the inclemency of the weather to which he was exposed in a third class carriage of the Great Western Railway Company', the weather being unusually severe for March. The jury recommended that the railway company provide additional closed accommodation for second and third class passengers, asking the Directors that the promise made at their last half yearly meeting to close those carriages be quickly carried out. Ironically, Sergeant Brown, a railway policeman at Bath, stated that a closed carriage was attached to third class trains, but the deceased's son said that his father was unaware that there was any coach for third class passengers other than the open one.

The 10.10am on which John Jonathan travelled was the outcome of Gladstone's Railway Regulation Act which had come into force the previous 1st November compelling the provision of at least one train a day each way at a speed of not less than 12 mph including stops, which were to be made at all stations, such a train having carriages protected from the weather and provided with seats. Fares were not to exceed a penny a mile. These were known as 'Parliamentary' trains.

Although the broad gauge had a number of advantages, such as allowing room for larger and more powerful locomotives, and making rolling stock more stable in the event of an accident, with the development of railways and the need for passengers and goods to travel from one part of the country to another, the break of gauge from a standard to a broad gauge line, with the cost of labour in transferring goods, the increased risk of breakage and delay in time, or the transfer of passengers with their mounds of luggage which they felt bound to take with them, proved quite unacceptable. It was not practicable for standard gauge lines to be altered to broad gauge, so the broad gauge either had to be completely converted or changed to mixed gauge. With the latter, a third rail was laid so that standard gauge trains could use one broad gauge rail and the inner third rail. In order that passenger coaches were close to platforms, the outer broad gauge rail was used by standard gauge trains. Mixed gauge came into use between Bristol and Bath in June 1874, this step having to be taken to accommodate trains from the Weymouth and Salisbury branches

The broad gauge *Tornado* stands at Bristol on mixed gauge track. She was built in 1888 and scrapped four years later with the abolition of the broad gauge. *Mrs J Willmott*

which had been converted to standard gauge. The first standard gauge trains between Swindon and Bristol ran on the afternoon of Sunday 21st June 1874, the nine-long empty coaching stock trains running via Trowbridge, as the section from Thingley Junction, west of Chippenham, to Bathampton was still broad gauge. The broad gauge rails between Bristol and Bath were used principally after this by Paddington to West of England trains, lines west of Exeter not being converted until May 1892. The very last broad gauge Down train to run between Bath and Bristol on Friday 20th May was the 5.00pm Paddington to Plymouth, hauled as far as Bristol by *Bulkeley* where it was replaced by the *Iron Duke*. The last Up broad gauge service train was the Night Mail which left Penzance at 5.00pm on that Friday and was scheduled to leave Bath at 1.30am on the Saturday. This was not the very last broad gauge train to travel between Bristol and Bath as all broad gauge rolling stock from the west had to be taken to scrapyards at Swindon by 13 special trains which passed through Bristol during the night. In addition to these through trains, some broad gauge coaches were placed in sidings at Exeter to be taken on to Swindon a little later,

as the mixed gauge east of Exeter was not immediately removed.

The railway first felt the attack from internal combustion-engined vehicles in February 1906 when the Bristol Tramways & Carriage Company started a Bristol to Keynsham service, cheaper than the rail journey, causing a decrease in GWR receipts of £48 in March and £49 in May.

GWR diesel railcars used the line in the late thirties, (a porter at Temple Meads when he saw one remarked, 'Here comes the dismal'), and BR diesel locomotives and diesel multiple-units started appearing at the end of the fifties. It is quite possible that before the end of the century the Bristol to London line will be electrified. As far back as 22nd March 1937 Philip M Crosse, a traffic consultant speaking to the Bath Chamber of Commerce, told of the benefits of electrifying the line. He said that there were 12 Up trains from Bath to Paddington and 15 Down. The fastest took 1hr 45m, the majority 2 to 2½ hrs and slow trains over 3hrs. Electricity would give a uniform 1hr 40m and the service could be doubled. The company would save money painting stations, and goods traffic would be speeded. He put the cost of electrification at about £300,000.

The very last Down broad gauge train leaving Swindon on 20th May 1892: the 5.00pm Paddington to Plymouth hauled by *Bulkeley*. The van behind the tender has a standard gauge body on a broad gauge underframe, thus making conversion a relatively easy matter. *Author's Collection*

The last broad gauge train to Penzance about to leave Paddington: the 'Cornishman' on 20th May 1892 behind *Great Western*. Notice the burnished buffers. *Author's Collection*

Description of the line from Bristol to Bath

Brunel took enormous trouble to ensure that the new railway blended with the existing landscape and was particularly fortunate that the Bristol Directors allowed him to build more decorative structures than their London counterparts. Large bridges and certainly all tunnel mouths and stations were designed for their unique situations. Brunel's standard over or under bridge between Bristol and Bath had a Tudor arch of 30-ft span, and this style was used for most of his structures. The terminus at Bristol, built on a field known as Temple Meads, is imposing and splendid, deliberately designed like a gentleman's country seat in order to give early travellers confidence in the railway. Thomas Osler, secretary of the Bristol Committee, wrote the following letter to Charles A Saunders, his London counterpart:

Great Western Railway Office,
Corn Street,
Bristol.
27th July 1839.

My dear Saunders,

With regard to the Bristol Temple Meads Station and the great importance of its economical construction, the Directors are persuaded it will be seen that every attention has been given to that essential object. So extreme was the anxiety felt on the first discussion of particulars that it was considered whether it would not be advisable to erect nothing more than a mere Wall in the line of the public road for the purpose, rather than any other, of concealing such plain buildings or sheds as would be indispensable to the temporary conduct of the business, leaving any erections of a more permanent character to be provided at a future period. On following out this idea, however, it was soon perceived that it would entail a long train of subsequent and considerable expense, as well as occasioning a very serious amount of practical inconvenience which would be obviated by at once proceeding to erect Buildings that, as far as they went, would be of permanent description. Brunel was instructed, therefore, to prepare plans of such offices only as were requisite and which were to be as devoid of ornament as was consistent with decent sightliness. In a week or two after he submitted a couple of Elevations. The first of his sketches exhibited a plain specimen of what I believe is now called the 'Tudor' style; the second – with the exception of an open arch end – consisted I think of as thoroughly naked an assemblage of walls and windows as could well be permitted to enclose any Union Poor House in the Country. A single glance at the two seemed to indicate that however agreeable the former might be to our tastes the latter was the thing for our pockets, but the Directors found, to their surprise, that the cost of the 'Tudor' front would exceed that of its Quaker companion by just £90. Now presuming the expense to be not materially different, many reasons presented themselves for preferring the Gothic Façade. It harmonized not only with the character of the Bridges, Archways, etc, already built from Bath westward, but with the peculiar features of better built specimens of Bristol Architecture generally, it required less expenditure of ground room and it enabled the making of any subsequent additions that may be found necessary when the line is at work without involving such violation of symmetry in an Italian design. The Tudor style was therefore selected and the Bristol Directors are persuaded that their London Colleagues will approve the preference.

Yours, dear Saunders,
Ever faithfully,
Thomas Osler

Temple Meads, constructed of Bath stone on brick arches 15 ft above ground level, had a train shed with an impressive timber cantilever roof, its 72-ft span unsupported by any cross tie or abutment. The weight was carried by octagonal iron piers set rather awkwardly close to the platform edge, thereby obstructing the movement of passengers. Matters were eased when the broad gauge was abolished and the platforms could be widened. The glazed roof was 220 ft long and the platforms extended for a further 200 ft in the open. At the terminal end of the station was a much lower ceiling supported by closely-spaced slender iron columns, this area forming the engine shed. Above and in front of this locomotive area was the four-storey office block and it was not unknown for steam and smoke to seep up through the floorboards. *Morgan's Guide*, published in

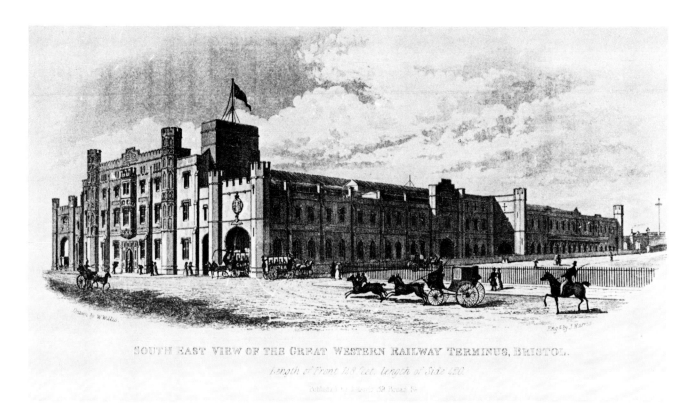

SOUTH EAST VIEW OF THE GREAT WESTERN RAILWAY TERMINUS, BRISTOL.

Frontage of GWR terminus: departure entrance, left; arrival side, right. A bus for Clifton is emerging with passengers off a train. Disc and crossbar signal on the far right. Flagstaff is on the water tower. Apart from the removal of the right hand gateway, the scene is much the same today. Engraving by J Harris, c1842.   *Author's Collection*

1849, captures the contemporary atmosphere of Temple Meads:

> A porter is ready to conduct you to the booking office, where you pay your fare and receive your ticket; you then ascend a flight of stairs to the platform. Having taken your place, and made all ready, you are now at ease to observe what is going on . . . several engines with red hot fires in their bodies, and volumes of condensed steam issuing from them; one of them moves slowly towards you. The huge piece bellows at first like an elephant: deep, slow and terrific are the hoarse heavings that it makes. It is then linked to the carriages . . . a whistle is sounded as a signal for starting – and you are off.

Facing Temple Gate was a symmetrical Tudor façade with the arms of the cities of Bristol and London, adopted by the GWR for its own arms, above the oriel window. There were flanking gateways, that on the departure side having a clock, while the right hand, or arrival side gateway was removed around the turn of the century. Luggage was carried up in lifts.

Departure side gateway, c1845.   *J C Bourne*

Bristol Temple Meads in the 1860s: Brunel's train shed, right; Bristol & Exeter Railway's offices, centre left; B&E terminal station, left. Note the cabs outside. Most of the railway tracks are mixed gauge. Several carriage and wagon turntables are in evidence for transferring stock to different roads. Two GWR horse-boxes stand beyond the coaches.

Author's Collection

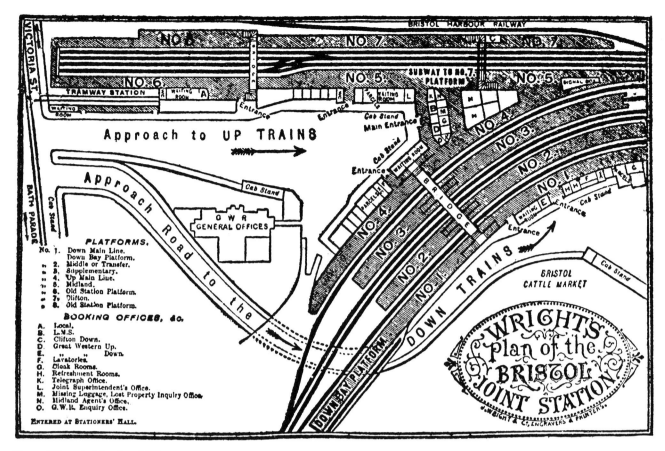

Plan of Temple Meads, c1910

From 1844 the Bristol & Gloucester Railway also used the station which was unable to cope satisfactorily with increasing traffic on all lines. A plan put forward in 1861 for a new central station in Queen Square was rejected by a narrow majority of the City Council. A solution had to be found, for just two platforms could not deal with GWR trains to and from London, Westbury and New Passage Pier, plus the Midland Railway (successor of the Bristol & Gloucester) services to Birmingham. The congestion led to Temple Meads not receiving a favourable press, the *Bristol Times & Mirror* commenting:

It would be difficult to find in all England a more rambling, ill-arranged and melancholy-looking group of buildings than those for the Midland, Great Western and Bristol & Exeter lines. The Midland and Great Western station makes a massive show outside; but the outside is delusive, for the accommodation provided by way of offices is of the smallest. It is really a punishment for a man to have to squeeze himself in among the crowds that assemble every day at the starting of almost every train,

in front of a single pigeon-hole that is used for the issue of tickets and for a lady, the difficulty of getting a ticket must be something dreadful. The Bristol & Exeter is certainly a trifle better in this respect than the others, but not much.

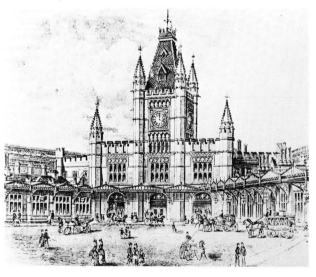

New entrance to Temple Meads, c1879. Original terminus is on the left.   *Author's Collection*

Temple Meads at 3.55pm in the early 1900s. In the centre is a GWR horse-drawn parcels van of a type which was still in use in the late forties, while early horseless carriages are beyond. Signs on the left direct people to the Midland Railway Parcels Office.
M J Tozer Collection

Taxi at the foot of Temple Meads station approach: terminal shed left, (with advertisement above windows for Anglo-Bavarian Ales & Stout); through train shed, right, with B&E offices on the far right.
M J Tozer Collection

Temple Meads at 1.42pm in the 1890s. Horse cabs stand beneath Francis Fox's canopy. The cabmen's shelter is in the centre.
Author's Collection

Tower wagon on Platform 4, 8th May 1987. *Author*

Memorial tablet to Emma Saunders at entrance to Temple Meads. She made herself responsible for the welfare of railwaymen. 4th September 1986. *Author*

The outcome of this was a decision to enlarge the existing station at Temple Meads and although Parliamentary authority was granted in 1865, disputes regarding the division of its cost took six years to resolve, while a further six were needed to carry out the work. The City Council did its part by building Victoria Street/Temple Street to give a better access to the station. A vast curved train shed, the span of 125 ft covering new through platforms, was built to the south of the original terminus, Vernon & Evans of the Central Ironworks, Cheltenham, being contractors for the metalwork. Sir Matthew Digby Wyatt, an old friend and colleague of Brunel, was the scheme's architect and made an excellent job of blending old and new. Brunel's original train shed was lengthened in similar style to the original, but using metal instead of wood. The enlarged station was officially opened on 1st January 1878, the pleasing sweep of the main entrance with its 100-ft high clock tower of Draycott stone approached up a gentle drive. Access to the Down platforms was by a road passing under the line to an entrance on the south, or Cattle Market side. Francis Fox of the Bristol & Exeter Railway designed the green and gold exterior canopy, virtually a copy of the one he did for the station at Weston-super-Mare.

Although a joint station, booking facilities were separate and passengers entered the Great Hall by different doors, a scroll above bearing the appropriate legend – the MR the left hand door; the B&E centre; and the GWR right.

Interior of Digby Wyatt's train shed before the removal of the centre platforms. This view, taken c1910, shows a Down Midland train at the centre platform, with a GWR express on the left. A staircase giving access to the footbridge from which this view was taken can be seen in the foreground.

M J Tozer Collection

Traffic grew still further, to such an extent that the station proved to be an inadequate size before it was fully completed. Plans for further extension were about to proceed in 1914 when World War One blocked them. By 1906, on occasions trains had stood block to block from Bath to Temple Meads on one side and Yatton to Temple Meads on the other. On post-war Bank Holidays, space was so inadequate that trains waiting for a platform were held in block from Highbridge. On summer Saturdays, local trains from Bath and Radstock took as long as 3hr 20m to travel the last mile into Temple Meads. The City Council had to take its blame for the frustration this caused as it had raised objections to the station being extended over the site of the Cattle Market.

To help ease the Depression, in 1929 the Government offered loans to carry out large public works, and the extension of Temple Meads qualified. P E Culverhouse drew plans to more than double the size of the station and provide all the main platforms with refreshment and waiting rooms. The work of extension involved widening bridges at both ends of the station from 62 ft to 312 ft. Foundations for these were made by West's Rotinoff Piling & Construction Co, 890 piles being driven and then faced with concrete to form a continuous wall which was then capped to carry the bridge.

New station buildings were of white or brown carrara bricks on a grey concrete plinth, the new platforms being sheltered by umbrella roofs, rather than an expensive train shed. In order to accommodate two shorter trains along one platform face, scissors crossings were provided between a platform and an adjacent through road so that a rear train could leave without being blocked by one in front. Shanks & McEwen of Glasgow, the main contractors, started work in November 1930, the task being finished in December 1935. Instead of a footbridge, a 300-ft long and 30-ft wide subway gave access to platforms, hairdressing saloons and baths, parcels being carried in electric trolleys along a separate subway, electric lifts connecting with the platforms. The new platforms were lit by gas, this form of illumination lasting right up to 1960 when fluorescent tubes were substituted.

Temple Meads, c1936, after completion of the extension. The spire above the entrance tower can be seen projecting above the roof of Digby Wyatt's train shed.   *M J Tozer Collection*

No 4060 *Princess Eugenie* heading the 11.25am Cardiff to Paignton in the late 1930s

An unusual visitor: SR 'Battle of Britain' class No 34079 *141 Squadron* about to leave Platform 9 with the Derbyshire Railway Society's special to visit Derby and Crewe Works on 14th June 1964.

Hugh Ballantyne

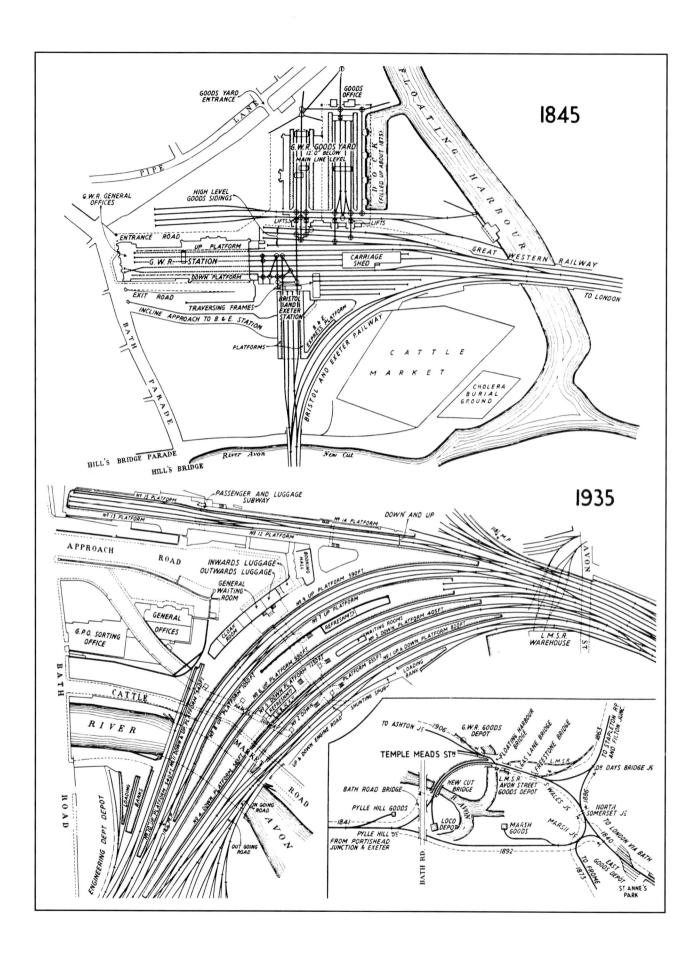

26

Crowds of spotters at Temple Meads on 5th September 1953. No 5982 *Harrington Hall* with a Down express is on the left and sister engine No 6972 *Beningbrough Hall* right with a Down stopping train. The loco yard signalbox is on the far right.

R.E.Toop

No 5000 *Launceston Castle* at Temple Meads with an Up train, 7th June 1952.   *R E Toop*

During World War Two enemy raiders were given Temple Meads as a target, but the station was never completely put out of action. On 6th December 1940 the 7.10pm to Salisbury received a direct hit in the station and there were heavy casualties, while on 3rd January 1941 incendiary bombs rained down and one lodged and lay undiscovered behind the clock tower, burning out the booking and parcels offices, tickets having to be sold from temporary accommodation in army huts hastily erected in the station approach.

In the sixties a reduction in the number of trains allowed an economy to be made by closing Brunel's terminal train shed to rail traffic on 12th September 1965, becoming a much-needed extension of the car park the following year. One of the oldest surviving terminal stations, it is a Grade 1 listed building and has recently been restored. In 1990 the roof of Wyatt's curved train shed was replaced at a cost of £2m.

Starlings and pigeons found Wyatt's shed a sheltered roosting place, but their droppings made them very unwelcome visitors. In 1969 nets were hung from the 75-ft high roof apex to just above railway vehicle roof level, deterring most of the birds.

Temple Meads had a Superintendent rather than a Stationmaster, the Superintendent being only responsible for operation and the fabric of the buildings; other duties undertaken by normal stationmasters were covered by independent men – Guards' Inspector, Parcel Agent and Passenger Manager. The post of Superintendent was filled alternately by a man from the GWR and the LMS. For example, W Orton (LMS) was succeeded by W Thick (GWR). When a new platform timetable was required, to save the task of writing everything out, necessary alterations were made to an old timetable and sent to the printer. The first time that this was done following Thick's appointment, one of the clerk's amendments was to delete 'Orton' and replace it with 'Thick'. When the proofs were returned by the printer the clerk was surprised to discover that 'Orton' had been printed in wide letters!

Porters were all GWR appointments and as they received an average of about £1 daily in tips, they were not at all eager to rise to the higher grade post of Shunter because when learning their new job they were only paid at porters' rates and so missed the tips. Because of this, there was always a shortage of shunters at Temple Meads.

If an LMS train was ready to leave Bristol and a connecting GWR train was late, the former was

The entrance hall's ecclesiastical-type architecture. The kink is imaginative: 'What wonders lie around the corner?' 4th September 1986. *Author*

trouble they had given him.

To avoid the expense of having a raised goods shed and tracks, the goods yard was situated at ground level, access being by wagon turntables and two hydraulically powered lifts. Each lift lowered one wagon and raised another at the same time, the two approximately counterbalancing. The operation of lowering a wagon through 12 ft took about half a minute. The goods shed, measuring 326 by 138 ft, was a fine functional Brunel design pleasing in appearance and capable of holding 209 wagons. Cranes were provided to aid unloading, while horses and hydraulic capstans were used for wagon movements within the shed so that the atmosphere remained unpolluted by locomotive fumes.

allowed to be delayed for a certain number of minutes. If it had to be sent on before the connection arrived, there were sometimes irate passengers to pacify. Wilfrid George Saunders, one time Chief Clerk, used good psychology and when passengers complained, politely asked, 'What can I do? I can't get the train back'. He offered to let them phone or telegraph anyone at their destination, at the railway's expense, to advise their new time of arrival. Additionally a cup of tea was given to soothe worried old ladies. After receiving this treatment, passengers often left his office quite pacified and apologising for the

Temple Meads at 10.42am on the 23rd February 1990. Little altered from the early days and perhaps even improved by the removal of the spire above the tower. *Author*

Bristol Temple Meads East signalbox, 26th March 1935.

GWR

The goods shed, like the passenger station, became inadequate to cope with increased traffic and between 1874 and 1876 was extended by Rowland Brotherhood, a Chippenham contractor. The barge dock was filled in, rail/water transfer being catered for at a new barge wharf. (Barges were used to transfer traffic between rail and ship, as, particularly in the early days, berths did not have rail access). As lift access to the goods shed caused unacceptable delays, the goods yard was raised 3 ft 6 ins and an incline built to connect the main line with the goods yard. The incline of 1 in 60 assisted with shunting as it made a natural hump. By 1914, between 1,600 and 1,700 wagons went in and out daily and 19 trains conveying a total of 600 wagons were despatched between 6.00pm and 6.00am. In due course this enlarged depot became inadequate and in 1924 a new goods depot costing £556,450 was built covering an area of over five acres and at the time was the largest covered area in Great Britain. It accommodated 408 wagons under cover and 330 more in the yard. Electrically-powered capstans moved wagons, and electric lifts gave access to the cellars for storing bacon, butter, cheese, lard and other perishables. The depot, latterly used by

National Carriers Limited, was demolished in 1982.

By 1909, the track layout at Temple Meads was controlled by four signalboxes, two of which contained 105 levers each. Coupled with the 1930s extension, Temple Meads East and South Wales Junction boxes were replaced by Temple Meads East power box, the largest on the GWR with no less than 23 block bells, each one of sufficiently different tone to enable a trained ear to decide which one was ringing. The box had three storeys, while the West and Loco boxes had only two. The architecture of all three, with their red brick in Flemish bond relieved by white stone sills and lintels, still looked modern when replaced 35 years later by a Multiple Aspect Signalling box situated at the mouth of Brunel's terminus. The East box had 368 levers and was continuously manned by three special class signalmen and a booking boy. Temple Meads West had 328 levers, 20 bells and was also manned by three men and a lad. In 1970, MAS operated from Bristol, controlling routes from Cogload Junction near Taunton through Bristol to Bradford Junction; to Corsham; Badminton; Charfield; Pilning and Avonmouth. This enabled 70 manual boxes to be closed, requiring 343 less staff.

View of the alterations at Bristol Temple Meads, 1934. Temple Meads West signalbox is in the foreground and the Bath Road crosses the rails on a girder bridge. *GWR*

Temple Meads goods depot, late 1920s.

Interior of Temple Meads goods depot.

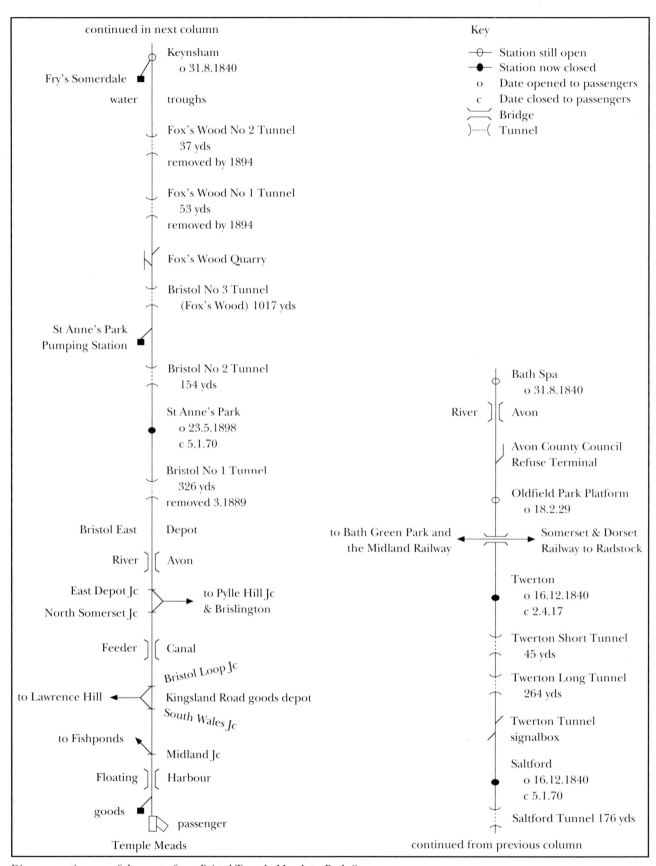

continued in next column

Key

○— Station still open
●— Station now closed
o Date opened to passengers
c Date closed to passengers
}{ Bridge
)---(Tunnel

Keynsham
o 31.8.1840

Fry's Somerdale

water   troughs

Fox's Wood No 2 Tunnel
37 yds
removed by 1894

Fox's Wood No 1 Tunnel
53 yds
removed by 1894

Fox's Wood Quarry

Bristol No 3 Tunnel
(Fox's Wood) 1017 yds

St Anne's Park
Pumping Station

Bristol No 2 Tunnel
154 yds

Bath Spa
o 31.8.1840

River }{ Avon

St Anne's Park
o 23.5.1898
c 5.1.70

Avon County Council
Refuse Terminal

Bristol No 1 Tunnel
326 yds
removed 3.1889

Oldfield Park Platform
o 18.2.29

Bristol East   Depot

to Bath Green Park and   Somerset & Dorset
the Midland Railway   Railway to Radstock

River }{ Avon

East Depot Jc
North Somerset Jc   to Pylle Hill Jc
& Brislington

Twerton
o 16.12.1840
c 2.4.17

Feeder }{ Canal

Twerton Short Tunnel
45 yds

Bristol Loop Jc

Twerton Long Tunnel
264 yds

to Lawrence Hill   Kingsland Road goods depot
South Wales Jc

Twerton Tunnel
signalbox

to Fishponds

Midland Jc

Saltford
o 16.12.1840
c 5.1.70

Floating }{ Harbour

goods

passenger

Saltford Tunnel 176 yds

Temple Meads

continued from previous column

Diagrammatic map of the route from Bristol Temple Meads to Bath Spa

Within the first mile of Temple Meads, Brunel had to design three major bridges to carry the Bath line over first the Floating Harbour – this bridge having two arches each of 56-ft span; the Feeder Canal – this was originally a timber structure, replaced by iron bow-string girders in 1879 which in turn were replaced by steel plate in 1965; and the River Avon. Leaving Temple Meads on a gradient of 1 in 264 down, junctions followed in quick succession: first the divergence of the Midland's line to Gloucester and Birmingham; then the triangle with the South Wales line formed by South Wales and Bristol Loop Junctions at the base and Dr Day's Bridge Junction at its northern apex. The Radstock branch diverged to the south at North Somerset Junction and nearly a quarter of a mile nearer Bath the main line is joined by the Bristol Avoiding line, 1 mile 6 chains in length, running direct from the Bristol & Exeter line at Pylle Hill, west of Temple Meads. On the south side of the main line is Kingsland Road goods depot. At present it has just two roads used for the temporary accommodation of locomotive-hauled Inter City coaches and will fall out of use as HST stock made redundant by ER electrification comes to Bristol for use on the WR and locomotive-hauled coaches will no longer be required. At one time Kingsland Road was a major depot with 23 roads, where among other traffic, about 60 wagons of coal were unloaded daily by grab for a nearby gasworks. The yard also dealt with livestock.

Beyond was Bristol East Depot, opened in 1890

No. of Siding.	Used for.	No. of Wagons Siding will Hold.
1	Wagons for transfer to down yard..	37
2	Spare vehicles and wagons for Clifton and Avonmouth Line ..	36
3	Newbury and beyond	35
4	Melksham, Holt Junction, and stations to Newbury (exclusive) ..	35
5	Reading, Acton, Old Oak Common, and Paddington	37
6	Swindon and stations to Didcot (inclusive)	34
7	Chippenham and Calne	33
8	Stations to Corsham	33
9	Oxford, Banbury, and L. & N.E. ..	33
10	Weymouth, Portland, and Easton ..	32
11	Stations Witham to Dorchester (inclusive)	31
12	Southern Railway, via Salisbury ..	31
13	Westbury and stations to Salisbury	31
14	Bradford-on-Avon and Trowbridge	30

Allocation of sidings in Bristol East Depot's gravitational yard, from *Great Western Railway Magazine*, 1923.

to cope with the extra traffic brought by the opening of the Severn Tunnel four years previously. Bristol's largest yard, East Depot had 18 roads on the Up side and 17 on the Down, the former being converted to a more economical gravitational yard on 7th October 1923, saving about 100 engine hours weekly. The Up yard dealt with 41 trains every 24 hours, an average of 1,300 wagons passing over the hump daily. Both yards

Bristol East Depot's gravitational yard, 1923

GWR

Engineer's sidings at Bristol East Depot. Notice what a vast amount of rock had to be excavated to attain the correct level. 17th March 1990.
Author

closed on 7th August 1967. The Down yard is now used by the Civil Engineer's wagons. Until about 1964, to the north of the Up yard, a private siding served John Lysaght Ltd's steel works, the company having its own locomotives for shunting. At the Bath end of East Depot the line enters a deep cutting with vertical walls. Originally Bristol No 1 Tunnel, 326 yds in length, the construction of shunting necks on the Up side involved its demolition and the widening of the resulting cutting. This work, completed on Sunday 31st March 1889 having taken a year, was carried out without interrupting traffic. When No 1 Tunnel was bored, two nodules, nicknamed 'the apple and the pear', were found in the sandstone and Brunel set them up near the east portal, though they have since been removed. When St Anne's Park was opened on 23rd May 1898 it took over from Keynsham the task of ticket collection, Temple Meads being 'open' until 1935. St Anne's Park, unstaffed from 6th March 1967, closed on 5th January 1970. It is said that the station was built from the stones of a prison situated between No 1 and No 2 Tunnels.

Train emerging from the west portal of Bristol No 1 Tunnel, c1845.
J C Bourne

36

View from near St Anne's Park station through the cutting, formerly Bristol No 1 Tunnel, towards Bristol East Depot. The curved signal gantry, supported only by the vertical sides of the cutting, was probably unique. The East Depot signalbox can be seen clinging to the side of the cutting at its far end. As the distant signals are red the picture is pre-1927.   *GWR*

Bristol East Depot signalbox supported on four girders let into the side of the cutting. The stairway is protected against falling rock.   *GWR*

Photograph, c1890, of mixed gauge track on a site later occupied by St Anne's Park station. The 'apple and the pear' can be seen on a plinth in the bottom right-hand corner. The western portal of Bristol No 2 Tunnel is top left.

St Anne's Park station, looking east to Bristol No 2 Tunnel. A Down stopping train departs, hauled by a 'City' class 4-4-0. The lane in the top left-hand corner is now First Avenue.

Author's Collection

West portal of Bristol No 2 Tunnel, c1845 showing the 'ruined' appearance.

J C Bourne

Bristol No 2, or St Anne's Park, Tunnel is 154 yds in length. Following a landslip during its construction which rendered a retaining wall unnecessary, its western portal was purposely left unfinished so that it resembled a ruined medieval

View, c1875, from the site of St Anne's Park station to the west portal of Bristol No 2 Tunnel. The track is mixed gauge.

Author's Collection

gateway, Brunel even planting ivy to increase the appearance of age. E Churton in *The Rail Road Book of England* published in 1851 said that it was 'so pleasing an object that it has long been considered one of the principal attractions of the neighbourhood'. The use of 'long' is interesting at a date when it had only been completed about a dozen years before. The eastern portal is of coursed stone with arch rings of blue brick. On 6th December 1940, a bomb fell near this mouth and damaged a coach of a Salisbury to Cardiff express.

Beyond No 2 Tunnel was St Anne's Park Pumping Station which supplied water to St Philip's Marsh and Bath Road locomotive sheds as well as Fox's Wood troughs. The Avon water was fairly good, but occasionally at times of very high tide there was a slight salt contamination. The pump was originally steam-powered, coal being brought by rail to an adjacent siding. Latterly an electric pump was fitted. During WW2 a bomb destroyed the filter and water was pumped direct, resulting in an eel spending three years in the water tank of an 0-6-0PT until it went to Swindon shops.

Between No 2 and No 3 Tunnels a massive retaining wall carries the line through the gorge on a shelf. No 3 Tunnel (Brislington) is 1,017 yds in length. Three shafts were used to bore it and six smaller shafts driven to carry off fumes from the blasting powder; after completion, five of these

No 3396 *Natal Colony* passing over Fox's Wood troughs, 25th February 1940. A water tank feeding the troughs is on the left. Although the engine is carrying express headlights it is, in fact, hauling an Up stopping train and behind the tender is a non-corridor 'B' set.

G H Soole

No 6023 *King Edward II* nears the end of Fox's Wood troughs on the 10.05am ex-Temple Meads to Bath – a train hauled by an ex-works engine, 11th June 1957.

Author

A Down train leaving Keynsham station, c1910. The overbridge beyond the station is typical of those on the Bristol to Bath section.

Keynsham: waiting shelter built 1985 on the Up platform. 17th March 1990.   *Author*

nine shafts were left open for ventilation. In sinking the shafts, slight interruption was caused by meeting old coal workings. The western entrance resembles a castle gateway; the eastern being left rough like a cave, although now being supported by an arch of engineer's blue brick. Being cut through hard rock it did not need lining like the others.

East of No 3 Tunnel, sidings lay both sides of the line, those to the south serving Fox's Wood Quarry. Stone from this quarry was used among other things for building the carriage shop at Swindon Works. The name 'Fox' was not from the quadruped, but a Quaker doctor, Edward Long Fox, who built Brislington House as a private asylum on a desolated stretch of land. He believed in a more humane treatment for the insane than was generally practised at that time, brass bands playing on the lawns being one of the entertainments provided. Before blasting, the quarry foreman was required to go to Fox's Wood signalbox and be given a brass disc as a token of authority and while the disc was in the foreman's possession, the signalman gave the 'Obstruction Danger' signal to boxes on either side and pegged the block telegraph to 'Train on Line' so that no train could pass and be at risk. The sidings were lifted in the 1950s.

Just east of Fox's Wood signalbox were Fox's Wood No 1 and No 2 Tunnels, 53 and 37 yds long respectively, and opened out by 1894. Beyond the

550-yd long water troughs, the line rises at 1 in 1,320 and passes on a high embankment over Keynsham Hams. The southern slope of the embankment carried 'Somerdale' in very large white capital letters to indicate the chocolate factory on the far side, the Great Western Directors probably drawing a line at 'Fry's' being added to turn the embankment into a gigantic advertising hoarding. During WW2 the lettering was camouflaged in order to deter the enemy from identifying where they were, as the letters would have been visible from the air. Keynsham station, known as 'Keynsham & Somerdale' from 1st February 1925, reverted to 'Keynsham' on 6th May 1974 and was unstaffed from 23rd May 1966. It had a two-storey stone building and due to the configuration of the land, had its back to the town. This structure was replaced by bus-stop type shelters until the station was jointly refurbished by BR and Avon County Council in 1985. This work also involved replacing the footbridge, the old one

⇌ Keynsham

Improvement works, completed in December 1985 at this station, including provision of a footbridge and enlarged car park, were funded jointly by British Rail and Avon County Council

being sent to Buckfastleigh for preservation on the Dart Valley Railway. The original small goods yard was at the east end of the station until a larger one opened further east in January 1911. This closed on 29th November 1965. From the passenger station, a line led to J S Fry & Sons Ltd's chocolate factory, the private siding being worked by a four-wheel vertical boiler geared Sentinel No 7492 built new in 1928 and sold to Grove Scrap Iron & Steel Merchants, Fishponds, Bristol in January 1964. It was assisted in later years by an 0-4-0 diesel-mechanical *Somerdale* built by Hudswell, Clarke & Co, No D1009, built 1956. The siding was taken out of use on 26th/27th July 1980. The factory also had a 1 ft 11¾ in gauge system. Nearer Keynsham goods yard, between 1932 and 1969. Keynsham Paper Mills was served by a private siding, the line being worked by one petrol and one diesel locomotive. Keynsham East signalbox, destroyed by fire on 16th May 1956, was replaced by another a month later. At the far end of Keynsham East complex, the Square Grip

Reinforcement Co (London) Ltd had a private siding from 1956 to 1966, as did Tate & Lyle from 1952 to 1966.

Saltford Tunnel, 176 yds in length, would have been longer but for a landslip when it was being cut which removed the necessity for part of the tunnelling. The portals are simpler than the rest on this length, just plain Tudor-Gothic arches.

The original Saltford station had timber buildings, but these were burnt down on 3rd August 1873 and rebuilt in stone. When the platforms were extended in 1909 over the site of the original signalbox, a new box was built at the other end to serve a goods yard which came into use on 9th November 1909. On 9th October 1941, a Whirlwind fighter aircraft crashed in the yard embedding itself in the weighbridge pit and killing the pilot. Saltford was latterly looked after by a porter under the Keynsham stationmaster. A stone built into the old brass mill not far away was crudely carved: 'Begun Diggin [*sic*] the Rail Road June 11 1836' referring to the cutting behind the

No 7015 *Carn Brea Castle*, ex-works, heads the 10.05am Bristol to Bath on 23rd November 1957. Saltford Tunnel is in the background.

Hugh Ballantyne

Saltford station, looking towards the tunnel. This picture was taken before 1909 when the platforms were extended and a goods yard brought into use.

M J Tozer Collection

Saltford station, looking east before the closure in 1909 of the signalbox on the right. Below its left-hand end window is a circular plate bearing the letter 'S' and a diamond plate bearing 'T'. These were used to indicate the state of the signal and telegraph equipment respectively. If a fault developed, the appropriate plate was reversed. The plates could be seen by inspectors or linesmen passing in trains. On the left on the far bank of the Avon is the Midland Railway's Mangotsfield to Bath branch. *GWR*

works. East of the station, the line becomes level and Saltford embankment begins. One and a half miles in length and 20 ft high, in one place it has a retaining wall where the Avon came to its door until diverted in the mid-1960s during a flood relief scheme. On the north side of the valley floor was the Midland Railway's Mangotsfield to Bath branch and as the two lines ran parallel within sight of each other for two miles, unofficial races sometimes took place.

The railway passes under the Bristol to Bath road by a skew bridge (known as Cross Posts Bridge in the early days) which was hit by a bomb on 25th June 1940, blocking road and railway. Beyond, the line enters Newton cutting. While this was being excavated, the remains of a large Roman villa, 125 ft by 55 ft, were discovered, at one time its tesselated pavement being preserved in Keynsham station. Now in the Bristol City Museum & Art Gallery, it is in thousands of pieces and too fragmentary to reconstruct.

The two sidings at Twerton Tunnel signalbox were added before 1890 to assist the line cope with additional traffic brought by the opening of the Severn Tunnel, because until the opening of the

Badminton line, all trains from the Severn Tunnel travelling to Swindon had to go via Bath in addition to those to Salisbury and Southampton. Trains could be reversed into one of these refuge sidings to enable a faster train to pass. Latterly, the Up refuge siding was used for storing coaches. Both sidings were taken out of use on 12th November 1950.

Twerton Long Tunnel, 264 yds in length, has a most attractive Tudor semi-elliptical arch with flanking towers like the entrance to a castle, the topography causing the eastern portal to be asymmetrical. Then follows a walled cutting and the 45-yd long Twerton Short Tunnel. Also Tudor-Gothic in style, it is unusual in being pointed throughout and having a remarkably flat arch. Beyond is Twerton Viaduct, 638 yds in length. Some of its arches were finished off as cottages but the vibration from trains above made them quite unsuitable for habitation so they were let as store sheds. This viaduct was struck in nine places by bombs during the three Baedeker raids on Bath in April 1942 and 100 ft of wall demolished. The Down line was temporarily supported by longitudinal timbers and soon re-opened, but the

No 4936 *Kinlet Hall* emerges from Twerton Tunnel into the evening sunshine on 1st September 1952 with a Swindon to Bristol train.

R E Toop

Ex-GWR twin diesel railcars Nos 35 and 36 on Twerton Viaduct working the 8.05am Bristol to Weymouth on 20th April 1954. The lower part of the viaduct was intended to be used as cottages. *Author*

Up line was not so easy to deal with. A crossover was inserted between the Up and Down tracks either side of the breach so that traffic could work both ways over a short stretch of the Down line. A temporary bridge to carry the Up line was constructed by driving in timber piles, this work being carried out by a 15-ton crane specially equipped with pile driving leaders and a steam hammer. The Up line was opened three weeks later.

Twerton owed its by-pass to the GWR, as a new road was constructed immediately north of the viaduct obviating the necessity for through traffic to pass through the village. As the railway cut through the lawn and garden of the vicarage, the GWR built a replacement parsonage further from the railway and nearer the church. Before the vicar moved into his new home, the railway building operations severed his sewers causing typhoid to break out and kill several of his children.

At the viaduct's east end was Twerton station, closed in 1917 as a wartime economy measure, since much of its traffic had been taken by Bath Electric Tramways which opened on 2nd January 1904. From 1st August 1899 it was named 'Twerton-on-Avon' to help distinguish it from Tiverton, as when handwritten, the two are very

similar – witness the number of photographs of 'Tiverton Tunnel' appearing in railway books.

On 5th July 1905, W T Tummy, stationmaster at Twerton, was suspended for cash irregularities, £17.8.5 paid to him on 31st May not being paid into the cashiers office, Bristol until 1st June! Further, in June and July, he under-remitted on some days, over-remitted on others. It was the practice for receipts from the GWR-owned Weston Lock, Bath, to be included with his cash and added to the two to three pounds of passenger receipts and the light income from the very small parcels traffic. Tummy had fallen into financial difficulties due to his standing surety for someone and subsequently was in the hands of money lenders. Tummy's trouble was compounded by the fact that his family, consisting of wife, eight daughters and a son, were constantly ill. The reason for this may have been revealed two years later when Tummy, then reinstated, complained of the poor condition of the station house due to dampness. This was because the track was on, or just below, the level of the bedroom, and water seeped from the track into the house wall. The GWR agreed that the building should be abandoned as a dwelling. The house had two

47

Twerton-on-Avon station, c1900. The platform extends over the skew arch. Notice the 3-storey house, at one time occupied by Stationmaster Tummy. *Author's Collection*

kitchens at ground level, two bedrooms below track level, sitting room at platform level and an attic above. Now in use as business premises, the station house still stands.

By the station house is a skew bridge of ashlar masonry built on the mechanically correct principle of spiral tapering courses, the bed-joints in every part of the arch being at right angles to the lines of pressure. By this method the arch does not depend for its stability on the friction and cohesion of the material, as it does to a great extent in very many skew bridges built in the usual way with spiral parallel courses, especially when the arches were semi-circular or semi-elliptical.

Steam railmotor leaving Twerton-on-Avon station for Bath, c1908. This Christmas postcard was postmarked on 24th December 1909. *Author's Collection*

'Barnum' class No 3222 passes under Brook Road, Twerton, with a Down stopping train, c1907, as a group of permanent way men stand aside. The overbridge is the standard type for the Bristol to Bath section.

Author's Collection

Grimy in appearance, No 2886 heads an Up coal train through Oldfield Park on 16th April 1963. Tickets were sold from the wooden cabin at the head of the steps on the left. *R E Toop*

The GWR passed under the Somerset & Dorset Railway's Bath Extension, opened on 20th July 1874. Oldfield Park Platform, opened in 1929 to serve a growing suburb of Bath, had two corrugated iron shelters on each platform and was a dreadful example of a station in this material. Its spartan appearance was heightened by the pleasing design of other stations on this line. A wooden ticket office originally stood by the entrance to the Down platform. Now unmanned, Oldfield Park has bus-stop type shelters. Traffic is increasing: in 1986 an average of 120 people per day used it, the figure now having increased to 300.

Beyond was Westmoreland Road goods depot with a large stone-built goods shed and most of the sidings to the north side of the line. Opened in 1877, it replaced an earlier depot adjacent to the passenger station. At the west end of the yard stood a single-road brick-built engine shed, a large water tank supported on independent cast-iron

columns forming the roof. The shed housed a shunting locomotive and also at various times either a steam rail-motor, or a small passenger tank engine. The engine shed closed in February 1961. Following damage caused by the Baedeker raids in April 1942, the weighbridge office, cement stores, Customs & Excise office and locomotive shed had to be rebuilt. This area of the former goods depot has now been redeveloped, but on the south side is a goods loop, an engineer's siding and an Avon County Council Refuse Terminal. Initially, ACC purchased 17 container wagons from Powell Duffryn. Five days a week a train is loaded with 8 containers at Bath and proceeds to the Great Western Refuse Transfer Station, Bristol where a further 22 are loaded, the remaining 15 being put on at Westerleigh, before proceeding to Calvert, Buckinghamshire, where their contents are disposed of in a landfill site, the train returning with empty containers.

'Castle' class No 5049 *Earl of Plymouth*, ex-works, leaves Oldfield Park with an evening stopping train from Swindon to Temple Meads on 16th June 1952. In the foreground, railwaymen have utilised the embankment for growing vegetables. This was common practice until about 25 years ago. *R E Toop*

Single car dmu No W55032 leaves Oldfield Park on 23rd October 1965 working the 2.37pm Temple Meads to Chippenham. Notice the poorly-designed corrugated-iron waiting shelter. *Author*

No 6000 *King George V* passes Bath goods yard with the 8.45am Saturdays-only Paddington to Weston-super-Mare on 28th July 1962. Behind the engine is Bath locomotive shed, with a water tank above. The bell on the locomotive's buffer beam bears the inscription: 'Presented to Locomotive King George V by the Baltimore & Ohio Railroad Company in commemoration of its century celebration September 24th–October 15th, 1927'.
Hugh Ballantyne

The 600-yd long, 73-arch St James' Viaduct had two interesting buildings below its eastern end – a mortuary and a police station. In 1902 Bath Corporation converted one of the arches into a mortuary and placed a carved inscription on a stone scroll over the entrance. It remained in use until 1948.

Brunel had intended making the skew bridge across the Avon immediately west of Bath station of iron and tenders for the 500 tons required were sought in May 1839, but due to delays the bridge was eventually built of timber, a material which allowed it to be constructed more quickly and also more cheaply than if he had constructed the arches of brick. It was his only laminated timber bridge and Bourne describes it in his *History of the Great Western Railway*.

The angle at which the Bridge crosses the River is so considerable that, although the space from quay to quay is only 80 feet, the space traversed by the railway is 164 feet. The bridge is of two arches, each of 80-ft span. Each arch is composed of six ribs placed about 5 feet apart and springing from the abutment and a central pier of masonry. Each rib is constructed of five horizontal layers of Memel timber held together by bolts and iron straps. The end or butt of each rib is enclosed in a shoe or socket of cast iron, resting with the intervention of a plate upon the springing stones, the shoes on the middle pier being common to the two ribs. The spandrils of the four external ribs are filled up with an ornamental framework of cast iron supporting the parapets. The interior ribs are connected by cross struts and ties. The cornice and parapet are both of timber; the latter is framed in open work of a lozenge pattern. The abutments are flanked by plain turreted piers, and the tow-path is carried on an iron gallery beneath the western arch.

This bridge was replaced by one of iron girders in 1877 and widened in the autumn of 1959 to allow the Up platform to be lengthened to hold 15 coaches. This could not have been done much earlier because hitherto a siding to the Bath electricity generating works was in the way. Because access to the works was by wagon turntable and therefore not available to locomotives, a shunting horse was used to haul wagons of coal to the power station. These sidings were on the site of the former goods shed, removed in the early 1890s. Dock sidings off the Down main were removed in 1960, allowing the Down platform to be extended to hold 10 coaches.

The general architecture of Bath Spa station is debased Elizabethan with Gothic windows and Romanesque ornaments. The principal front, of asymmetrical design with three gables and an oriel window, was flanked by curved wing walls

The north façade of Bath station, April 1931. An extension on the right in yellow brick contrasts with the Bath stone of the original. The bridge to the Royal Hotel can just be seen on the left, and electric tram tracks in the foreground.   *GWR*

Bath station from Beechen Cliff, c1890, showing the overall roof. Centre left is the old goods shed.

Author's Collection

forming a circular carriage sweep. Pleasing radial fan lights were set above the door openings. The peculiarity of the station at first was the 40-ft span roof supported at the sides by large iron columns inconveniently placed within 4 ft of the platform edge. The roof timbers were like long arms of cranes which met in the centre, short arms being held down by the side walls behind the platforms. Brunel adopted this design to avoid an outward thrust on the walls which were built on arches, the only other solution being to use cross ties which he wanted to avoid. There were four roads within the train shed, those in the centre being used as sidings and for run round purposes. Until its closure in November 1880, a single-road engine shed was sited at the Up end of the station. In 1897 the overall roof was removed and the platforms lengthened, an Up bay platform being added, but even so, accommodation was still limited, the Down holding 8 coaches, the Up 9, and the Bay 4. During World War Two, when expresses often comprised 16 coaches, a train had to draw up twice. In the blackout this caused an accident when a serviceman stepped on to a bridge girder thinking it was the platform, and then fell into the Avon. Another wartime mishap occurred during the Baedeker raids in April 1942 when a bomb destroyed part of the east end of the Down platform and canopy, blocking four tracks.

Because of the curve, on long trains the guard's 'Right Away' was difficult to see, so to overcome this problem lights marked 'RA' were fixed in 1947 to the ends of the platform and illuminated by the guard pressing a plunger. One of the station's central roads was taken out of use on 25th November 1962 and the other, together with the bay platform, on 31st March 1967.

One of the trains which used the latter was the 10.05am from Temple Meads, usually drawn by an ex-works engine which backed in to allow the Portsmouth train to pass. While he was waiting, a driver took the opportunity to oil round his engine. On one occasion he noticed the platform inspector leaning against the tender – a rather dandy character, sporting a button hole. This driver saw the inspector's shoe not far away and at a most convenient level on this platform. The opportunity was too good to miss. He poured oil into the inspector's shoe until it was full. The Portsmouth train came in and the inspector, quite oblivious of what had happened, took one step and then knew. He was certainly none too pleased with the driver.

Bath signalbox placed unusually above the platform canopy. 7th June 1963. *Author*

Due to the cramped nature of the site, one of the station's unusual features was the signalbox high above the Down platform awning which closed on 21st January 1968. From 1845 until 26th January 1936 an open girder footbridge made a direct connection between the Up platform and the Royal Hotel. Giuseppe Garibaldi, Italian patriot and hero, once planned to speak to the people of Bath from this bridge but the crowd of dignitaries greeting his train prevented him from leaving his carriage.

The first cloakroom for passengers' left luggage was introduced by the GWR. It was opened at Bath on 13th July 1846. The articles were kept separately and locked up, a printed receipt being given to the passenger depositing luggage who was charged twopence an article. A week later the Directors ordered the room to be abandoned, although the *Bath Chronicle* reported it a great success and well-patronised.

BRITISH RAILWAYS
WESTERN REGION

UNTIL FURTHER NOTICE

CHEAP DAY TICKETS
will be issued as shewn

ON WEEKDAYS and SUNDAYS
(Where train service permits)

BY ANY TRAIN

from BATH SPA

TO	RETURN FARES		TO	RETURN FARES	
	First Class	Third Class		First Class	Third Class
	s. d.	s. d.		s. d.	s. d.
BOX	1 10	1 0	KEYNSHAM & SOM.	2 5	1 5
BOX (Mill Lane)	2 1	1 3	LIMPLEY STOKE	2 4	1 5
BRADFORD-ON-AVON	3 3	2 1	PORTISHEAD	8 0	4 11
BRISTOL (Temple Meads)‡	3 11	2 5	ST. ANNE'S PARK	3 4	2 1
CHIPPENHAM	4 6	2 9	SALTFORD	1 5	0 11
CLEVEDON	9 2	5 7	SEVERN BEACH	8 2	4 11
CLIFTON DOWN	5 0	3 0	SWINDON	10 2	6 1
CORSHAM	3 1	1 11	TROWBRIDGE	4 6	2 9
DEVIZES (via Seend)	7 11	4 9	WARMINSTER	7 4	4 6
FRESHFORD	2 7	1 7	WESTBURY	5 10	3 6
FROME	7 6	4 6	WESTON-SUPER-MARE	10 7	6 4

from BATHAMPTON

TO	RETURN FARES	
	First Class	Third Class
	s. d.	s. d.
BATH SPA	0 11	0 6
BRISTOL (Temple Meads)‡	4 9	2 10
CHIPPENHAM	3 9	2 4
TROWBRIDGE	3 7	2 2

PASSENGERS RETURN BY ANY TRAIN THE SAME DAY.

‡ Passengers have the option of returning from Bristol (Stapleton Road) by direct trains.

Excursion leaflet, January 1950

Bath station was one of the earliest to use platform tickets, these being required from 6th February 1913. Issued from two automatic machines costing £40 each, profits from the first day's takings were 15s 9d. The following month the remarkable figure of 12,019 tickets were sold bringing in an income of £50.1.7. Luggage lifts at Bath Spa were operated by hydraulic power, the header tank being at the east end of the Down platform below the tank supplying the locomotive water cranes.

The GWR built Dorchester Street and Manvers Street to give access to its station. Half of Dorchester Street was already in existence, but Manvers Street was new and had to be kept in

repair by the company until two-thirds of it had been lined with buildings when the responsibility then fell on the landowner, Lord Manvers. Early in 1922, No 8 Lyncombe Hill was purchased by the GWR at a cost of £890 for use by the stationmaster.

Advertisement in the *Bath & Wilts Chronicle & Herald*, 26th March 1934.

2. Bristol to Pilning and Yate via Filton

As the crow flies, Bristol is only 25 miles from Cardiff, but at one time the quickest way between the two cities was to travel by rail via Gloucester – a distance of no less than 93 miles! A short cut was needed. The first attempt at this was made in April 1845 when the Bristol & South Wales Junction Railway was mooted. Eighteen months later, its promoters bought the rights of the Old and New Passage ferries across the Severn to link with the Gloucester to Newport line opened in 1852. The BSWJR was wound up in 1853, but the idea was certainly not abandoned.

The following year a proposal was put forward to build a line from Bristol via Hotwells, Shirehampton and New Passage, there crossing the Severn by means of a floating bridge. That idea, too, was abortive, but the third attempt, the Bristol & South Wales Union Railway, succeeded. Parliament passed the necessary Act on 27th July 1857 granting powers for a railway between South Wales Junction, a quarter of a mile east of Temple Meads, to New Passage Pier, from where a ferry would run to Portskewett Pier on the other side of the river across two miles of water. The 11½ miles of single line were to be broad gauge.

Rowland Brotherhood of Chippenham began construction in October 1858. In carrying out his various contracts, Brotherhood required the use of locomotives and these were difficult to move about from one part of the country to another. To obviate this problem, Rowland's son, Peter, designed an engine capable of travelling on either road or railway and in 1862, one of these 11-ton machines travelled from Chippenham via Acton Turville and Iron Acton to the Bristol & South Wales Union Railway at Patchway over ordinary roads at an average speed of 6 mph.

Building a railway is not just a matter of scooping earth out of cuttings and tipping it to make embankments; problems can arise such as those detailed by Charles Richardson, a pupil of Brunel and engineer in charge of building the BSWUR. Above Ashley Hill station the railway was to cross a valley by an embankment 52 ft in height. He wrote:

A four-foot culvert had first to be put in under the deepest parts of it to carry the brook, which is liable to sudden floods. When the contractor had got out the ground for the foundation of this culvert, the bottom was so bad that he did not know what to do. On inspection I found that the bottom was lias clay, in which the foot sank ankle deep at every step; and a trial-pit sunk near it, showed that the same stuff went down for thirty feet. The question was, How could a culvert be built upon that bottom to carry a load of a 52-feet bank? I felt it to be a serious, momentous and nervous question: for if that culvert should collapse after the bank had been made, it would, of course, be after heavy rains when it would be running full of water. The heavy bank would follow the arch and choke the culvert. This big bank might thus form a dam across the valley, against which the water would rise, making a great reservoir of the valley above, until such time as it had accumulated sufficient force to cut a passage through the upper part of the bank. And this passage, though small at first, once made, would rapidly scour, until the water in a great body would burst through and suddenly discharge a flood, through the centre of Bristol into the Floating Harbour!

The valley bottom is narrow, and the sides rise, on either side, at a steep slope. The railway crosses this valley very much askew, so that the culvert was a very long one. But though the clay would slip in any available direction under such a load, I had ascertained that there was no compressible material, such as peat, mixed with it. I decided to build the culvert upon the bad bottom as it was, only covering it with a coating of lime and concrete, which enabled the men to stand up on it, and then to load the slip clay adjacent to the culvert, so that this clay could not be shoved out laterally. For this latter purpose I had a little more land bought, and lengthened the culvert about thirty yards at each end. A very strong four-foot barrel culvert, 2 ft 6 in thick, was then built, to the full length, of roughly-dressed stones, all set in good lias mortar. The culvert was nearly 140 yards long; daylight could not be seen through it owing to a sag in the middle, as Mr Benedict found out when he had to crawl through it.

The whole breadth of the valley bottom from slope to slope, was then covered with a thickness about four yards in depth of lias clay from Ashley Hill cutting, making a sort of level platform across the bottom of the valley, upon which the bank, forty feet higher, might be tipped without fear later on, after this platform had become consolidated. There still remained a very weak place in this embankment. The forty feet of bank above the platform, before the level of the next cutting was attained, had to be made over slippery ground, which could not carry even five feet without slipping very badly. This I decided to remedy by efficient deep drainage and a deep drain was therefore started from just above the level of the brook, at the upper end of the long culvert, and carried forward just inside the railway fencing, 2 ft 6 in wide, and with upright sides supported by horizontal planks and short struts. When this drain had attained a depth of full forty feet, a copious spring of water was tapped. Two six-inch pipes were then laid along the bottom of the drain, and it was filled to the top with loose stones, the planks being withdrawn as the stone got up to them.

On each bank of the Severn a pier was built of timber on a stone base. Designed by Charles Richardson, it is interesting to observe that while engaged on building these piers, he was led to consider the project of making a tunnel beneath the Severn. Trains ran to the ends of the piers, stairs taking passengers to pontoons of hulks moored alongside. The ferry steamers were able to land passengers at any state of the tide, despite rises of as much as 46 feet. Steam-operated lifts took merchandise and livestock to the correct level. The pier at New Passage was 1,635 ft long, while Portskewett was nearer deep water and needed to be only 708 ft in length. Each pier had its own hotel and private gas works.

At last the railway was ready for the ceremonial opening on Tuesday 25th August 1863. The special train stood in the platform at Temple Meads. The leading carriages were occupied by the band of the Bristol Volunteer Artillery which played a selection of appropriate music before the train started and as it moved out of the station. The line could not be opened to the public because the Board of Trade inspector, although satisfied with the line itself, required minor alterations to the fences. The *Bristol Mirror* was bitter.

> It would have occurred to a commonsense mind that so eminent a contractor as Mr Brotherhood might have been entrusted with the fulfillment of such an alteration, and the certificate be given at once. But the inspector chose to be punctilious and insisted upon further inspection. When the line was completed, it was stated he had gone to Scotland on business, although we must not omit to remark that grouse shooting is just now very popular.

The line was eventually opened to the public on Tuesday 8th September. The workings of the official mind were as curious then as they are today. The *Bristol Mirror* again reports: 'Strange as it may seem the Board of Trade, after having blocked up the line for a fortnight, at a heavy loss

New Passage Pier & Railway on the ceremonial opening day, 25th August 1863.   Courtesy *Illustrated London News*

to the proprietors, and a serious inconvenience to the public, sent word to the directors on Saturday, that the line might be opened for traffic without any re-inspection.' As it was usually the case with relatively minor railways, the company did not purchase its own locomotives and rolling stock, but had its line worked by a larger railway – in this case the Great Western. The coaches used were 'comfortable and commodious' and had been used underground on the Metropolitan Railway which had been worked by the GWR, but ceased owing to a disagreement between the companies.

The first Sunday excursion over the new railway was run on 13th September when more than 1,500 passengers were carried from Bristol to New Passage in a train of 21 coaches. On the return journey it stalled in Patchway Tunnel, the locomotives not being able to tackle the gradient with such a heavy load. In the 1870s, New Passage enjoyed the popularity which Severn Beach had in the 1930s. The GWR absorbed the BSWUR on 1st August 1868 and converted it to standard gauge in August 1873. 33 hours were allotted for the task, but it was completed within 28. Men were allowed to take the usual mealtimes, but food had to be taken to them. Each gang of 20 men had one man to cook their food and serve their needs. The railway company allowed them as much oatmeal as they could take, but no intoxicating liquor was permitted.

Most of the line could be used by trains to and from the Severn Tunnel and while this was being cut, to cope with the expected increase of traffic once it was opened, the section from Narroways Hill Junction to Patchway was doubled by a new Up line being built. This was first used on 1st September 1886, the day the tunnel was opened to goods traffic. As the Up gradient of 1 in 68 between Pilning and Patchway Tunnel was undesirable on such an important route, it was decided to build a new Up line some three miles in length between Pilning and a point south of Patchway station, the new line having an easier gradient of 1 in 100. It opened on 10th August 1885 in preparation for the completion of the tunnel. Down trains continued to use the original steeper line.

During the latter half of the last century, people often jokingly said that the initials 'GWR' stood for 'Great Way Round' and certainly many of the Great Western's main lines were far from being direct. When the Severn Tunnel was first used by passenger trains in 1886, expresses from London to South Wales had to curve southwards at Wootton Bassett, pass through Bath and Bristol and then bear northwards again to reach the tunnel. Trains were obviously travelling an unnecessary mileage and a direct link was needed through the southern end of the Cotswolds between Wootton Bassett and Filton. Coupled with the criticism of indirectness was the fact that many people in South Wales were highly dissatisfied with the service that the Great Western provided and threatened to build an entirely new railway from Cardiff to Andover where trains could run over the London & South Western Railway to London.

The GWR countered this threat to its South Wales traffic by proposing the Bristol & South Wales Direct Railway. This 31-mile long line from Wootton Bassett to Filton had several advantages. It shortened the distance from South Wales to London by ten miles; avoided two steep inclines enabling engines to pull twice the load; shortened the distance from Bristol to London by a mile; and reduced the number of trains on the Bristol to Bathampton section over which traffic had increased since the opening of the Severn Tunnel. James C Inglis, chief engineer of the GWR, piloted the Bill with such skill that no opposition was encountered in the Parliamentary Committee stage. The estimated cost of the $33\frac{1}{2}$ miles of line was £1.3m. The Act was passed in 1896 and the contract for construction let to S Pearson & Son early the following year.

The first through goods train to use the line left Bristol at 8.30am on 1st May 1903 – it being current practice for freights to consolidate the earthworks before passenger trains travelled over them. The first passenger train, the 6.32am, used the line two months later on 1st July. It carried the Superintendent of the Bristol Division of the GWR and several company officials, but there was no special opening ceremony, though children at most schools along the line were given a holiday. Four new direct expresses from Paddington to South Wales were run over the line. Its opening meant that there were now three routes from Bristol to London:

the original via Bath and Swindon $118\frac{1}{2}$ miles
via Bath and Devizes $121\frac{3}{4}$ miles
via Badminton $117\frac{1}{2}$ miles

The time taken by trains climbing the gradient of 1 in 75 in the section between Narroways Hill Junction and Filton caused considerable delay. To ease congestion and at the same time help relieve unemployment the line was quadrupled, two main tracks being laid east of the original lines which became relief. The work of quadrupling was

Horfield Station, also showing new double-arch overbridge.

Ashley Hill Station.
The other pair of lines are on the right, out of sight, between the platforms.

Bedminster Station.
This view gives a good idea of the long bay platforms.

Three stations in the Bristol district which have been reconstructed in connection with the quadrupling of running lines on both sides of Temple Meads Station.

Page from a 1943 *Great Western Railway Magazine* illustrating the quadrupling of the lines from Temple Meads; to the north, Horfield and Ashley Hill stations, to the south, Bedminster. *GWR*

The Severn Tunnel entrance, English side. Notice the large stone blocks used for constructing the portal. Beside Milepost 11 (distances from South Wales Junction, Bristol), by the permanent way men's hut, is a white post bearing markings showing that the Severn Tunnel is maintained by Gang No 33. Two men are sharpening an implement on a grindstone – one turning the handle while the other holds the tool.

M J Tozer Collection

completed on 30th April 1933. Modern traction has rendered the extra lines superfluous and it has now been restored to a double track section.

The opening of the loop at Westerleigh Junction, south of Yate, caused something of a rumpus. It came about because the Great Western had running powers from its line at Standish over Midland metals to Bristol. Then when the Bill for the Bristol & South Wales Direct Railway came before Parliament, a branch was proposed from Chipping Sodbury on the new line to Berkeley, where it would have made a junction with the Severn & Wye Joint Railway. The Midland opposed this scheme and the GWR withdrew it, agreeing instead to build loops to join the Midland at Yate and another to join the Severn & Wye near Berkeley Road. These loops were opened on 9th March 1908.

The GWR realised that it could now run a direct express from Wolverhampton to Bristol by using its running powers over the Midland from Standish and then regain its own line by the new loop at Yate. This was where the trouble began.

On 1st July 1908 the GWR started this new express, running in competition with the Midland's own trains. The MR did not intend to let the GWR provide opposition and claimed that the Yate connection was only authorised as a route to Sharpness or the Severn Bridge, and could not be used to facilitate competition between Birmingham and Bristol. The MR asserted that the new expresses should keep to the Midland all the way into Bristol and travel via Mangotsfield paying the additional toll for the extra ten miles. This the GWR did until November, almost invariably finding that a slow, even for the Midland, stopping train was in the long block sections just ahead of its express. In November the case came to court and the Midland lost. The Great Western was able to use its own track south of Yate, the Court of Appeal deciding that the whole included any parts and that it was quite in order for the GWR to run trains just from Standish to Yate over the Midland's track. The following summer the GWR introduced two more expresses over this route.

Description of the line from Bristol to Pilning and Yate via Filton

Leaving the Bath line at South Wales Junction just east of Temple Meads, the Filton line curves past the site of the original GWR engine shed to Dr Day's Bridge Junction where the direct line from St Anne's Park, avoiding Temple Meads, comes in. The junction's curious name arose because Dr William Edward Day lived in Barrow Road and when the South Wales line was cut, the bridge required was named after him. At its maximum extent, Dr Day's Carriage Siding had 21 roads. Out of use for coaches by 1969 it was used for vans and 'cripples'. The nearby Barton Hill repair shops are now one of only two in England maintaining parcels vans; they also repair engineer's wagons.

Lawrence Hill was originally a two-road station until the line was quadrupled from Dr Day's Bridge Junction to Stapleton Road in August 1891, the work being necessary to cope with increased traffic brought by the Severn Tunnel. A new enlarged goods depot opened in 1895. Beyond the station the line passed under the Midland Railway. Stapleton Road became the main Bristol station for Cardiff to Portsmouth trains which in steam days did not generally call at Temple Meads because of the need to reverse. There is a two-mile climb at 1 in 75 from Stapleton Road to beyond Horfield. Some trains stopped at Stapleton Road to take on rear end assistance and for this purpose two banking engines were kept there. The bankers were not required to be coupled so trains did not have to stop at Filton Incline box where bankers dropped off and crossed to return on the Down line.

Just north of Stapleton Road the line to Clifton Down and Avonmouth curved westwards at Narroways Hill Junction to Ashley Hill Junction line. Ashley Hill station closed in 1964, as did Horfield Platform which opened in 1927 and had its name simplified to 'Horfield' in November 1933. The rising gradient of 1 in 75 ends beyond the station and is followed by a fall at 1 in 300. Before Filton Junction is the Western Fuel Company's coal concentration depot which uses some of the sidings of the goods yard closed in 1965. Two private locomotives shunt the sidings. The original Filton station was just beyond and sited immediately south of the railway bridge over

Narroways Hill Junction: Filton line straight ahead, Avonmouth line left. View from the cab of a dmu, 14th June 1988. *Author*

Stapleton Road. c1910.

64

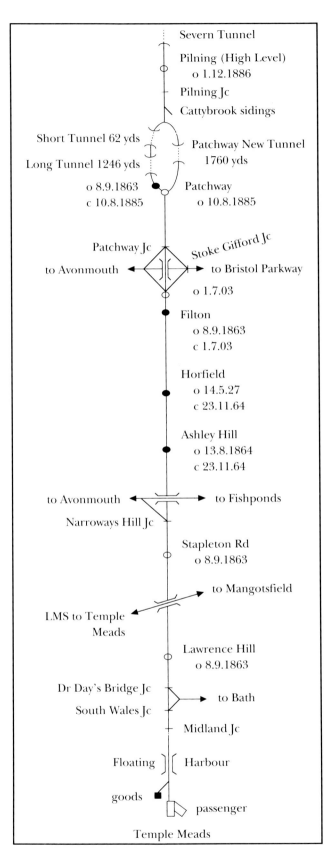

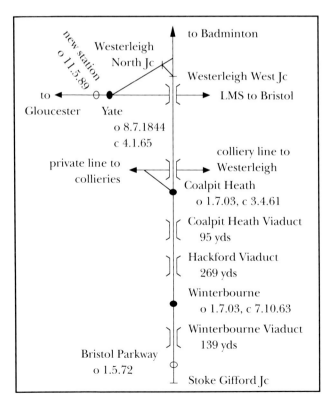

Diagrammatic map of the route from Bristol Temple Meads to the Severn Tunnel

Diagrammatic map of the route from Stoke Gifford Junction to Yate

Up stopping train arriving at Ashley Hill, c1910.

London & South Western Railway train set No 410 leaving the rural Ashley Hill station for South Wales, c1910. The lad by the signalbox is bowling a hoop. Beyond the signalbox is a greenhouse for growing bedding plants for the station garden. Opposite the signalbox is a corrugated-iron oil store.

M J Tozer Collection

A group of girls from the nearby Muller's Orphanage, on Ashley Hill platform awaiting a train to Bristol. *M J Tozer Collection*

the present A4174 ring road and was replaced by a new station with four platforms to the north of the ring road, this newer station being opened in 1903. Here the tracks diverge to Badminton and Avonmouth, the Severn Tunnel line continuing ahead. With the opening of a direct line from Filton to Avonmouth, the station was renamed Filton Junction, reverting to its original title on 6th May 1968. The Badminton line curves along the east side of the triangular junction and joins the line from the Severn Tunnel.

A marshalling yard was opened at Stoke Gifford in 1903 to relieve shunting at the various Bristol depots. The Up yard had 14 roads and the Down yard 10 roads. The 'Irish Mail via Fishguard Express', without stopping, slipped two coaches at Stoke Gifford East signalbox and these were taken to Temple Meads in order to provide a late evening service. With the accent on through loads, less shunting was required and the marshalling yard closed on 4th October 1971, the site being used for a new passenger station with extensive parking. Originally having unsheltered platforms, its facilities have been improved over the years as traffic has developed. Bristol Parkway

has proved a great success, convenient both for passengers living on the north side of Bristol wishing to use Inter City trains, and for motorists from the Bath area requiring to travel north who can drive to the station, use the car park (which at the time of writing is still free), and board a train there, often taking less time than changing at Temple Meads.

East of the station a bridge over the M4 is an example of a fairly rare welded portal frame type with uncovered steelwork. Its main girders are each 254 ft in length. The line passes over the 5-arch, 45–85 ft high, 139-yd long Winterbourne Viaduct, past the site of Winterbourne station and immediately on to Hackford Viaduct, 269 yds long, with 11 spans, 60–90 ft high. Coalpit Heath Viaduct, 95 yds in length, was situated before the station of that name. From here, between 1904 and 1949, a colliery siding ran to Frog Lane, Mayshill and Nibley collieries. During WW2, Frenchay Hospital, built for American war wounded, had its patients brought by ambulance trains to Coalpit Heath station.

A story runs that at one time the authorities, concerned about the great number of births at

A 4-4-0 locomotive hauling an express climbing through Ashley Hill station, c1910. The train's two centre coaches are London & North Western Railway stock. The background is dominated by Muller's Orphanage. The postcard was designed to be sent at Christmas. *M J Tozer Collection*

Construction of a railway bridge over Muller Road. Strollers watch the work progress. The embankment has been tunnelled through in order to lay the abutment walls, then girders are slung across as is being done in the photograph. *M J Tozer Collection*

2-4-0 No 3228 passing Patchway with an Up van train, c1912.

Author's Collection

Coalpit Heath, sent an inspector to investigate. At the *Ring o' Bells* a man, pushing his empty glass towards the official, said he knew the answer. His glass replenished, the man divulged that the culprit was Driver X. The inspector was aghast. 'He couldn't possibly have produced all those babies!' The man explained, 'Well, it's like this. He drives a goods train from Gloucester to Stoke Gifford and when he arrives at Frampton Cottrell, he likes a nice hot breakfast ready for him. His wife is a little bit deaf, so he blows the engine whistle from before Coalpit Heath station to Winterbourne. He wakes up the others as well. It's too early to get up; too late to go to sleep again, so they think of something else to do!'

The Badminton line crossed the Midland Railway and at Westerleigh West Junction, the Yate line curved round the west side of what was a triangular junction (the east side had a most chequered history and was closed and re-opened on a number of occasions, finally being closed on 4th January 1950), joining the Midland just south of Yate station.

In preparation for the introduction of High Speed Trains between Wootton Bassett and Stoke Gifford, a blanket of sand and polythene sheeting was put down before new stone ballast was laid, in order to prevent wet clay from pumping up into the ballast under pressure of passing trains. Rain can trickle through the ballast to the polythene and then run away to new trackside drains. The line closed for track relaying between 5th May and 6th October 1975, trains being diverted via Bath.

Continuing north from Filton station to Patchway station, the Severn Tunnel line descends a gradient of 1 in 90/68 to Pilning. The Up line (constructed when the line was doubled) was built with a more gentle gradient of 1 in 100 and because the two tracks were at different levels at the site of the original Patchway station, when the line was doubled the second station was built closer to Bristol. This second station opened as Patchway & Stoke Gifford but was renamed Patchway on 27th October 1908. The Down line has two tunnels: 1,246 yds and 62 yds in length respectively, while the Up road has one of 1,760 yds – exactly one mile. The ear drums tend to buckle when going into Patchway Tunnel on a Down train. The southern portal bore the plaque now preserved at Temple Meads: 'Bristol & South Wales Union Railway & Steam Ferry. Opened September Eighteen Hundred & Sixty Three. Christopher James Thomas, Chairman. Railway & Piers designed by Isambard Kingdom Brunel'. When the tunnel was being cut, the contractor, Rowland Brotherhood, impressed by the quality of the clay, used it for making bricks. The line's engineer, Charles Richardson, also struck by their

Pilning station, looking Up, c1910. Notice the wooden platform, attractive wooden seat and gas lamps.   *M J Tozer Collection*

No. ____________

Great Western Railway.

This form of application to be used for all men entitled to overtime allowances except Goods Guards who must continue to use form No. 1,693.

(645)

PILNING *Station.*

Name W E Turner *Grade* Porter

Cabin Station 12 *Hour post.*

Particulars of Duty for Week ending April 18th/97

DAY.	Booked Time. On. am	Booked Time. Off. pm	Actual Time. On. am	Actual Time. Off. pm	Over-time. H.	Over-time. M.	Cause of Overtime.
Monday ...							
Tuesday ...							
Wednesday							
Thursday ...							
Friday ...							
Saturday ...							
Sunday ...	8.15	8.15	8.15	8.15	12	0	Sunday duty
				Total	17	0	

Rate of Pay 17/– *per week.* *Time allowed* 3rd *Days.*

Amount entered for Overtime.	£	s.	d.
		2	10

F C Carr *Station Master.*

____________ *Superintendent.*

Applications for overtime must be forwarded to the Station Master, who, on satisfying himself that the amount claimed is correct, will sign this Sheet and forward it to the Superintendent, who, if he can allow the amount claimed, will attach his signature and return the Sheet to the Station Master, who will enter in the next Pay Bill the amount allowed by the Superintendent This Sheet must be attached to the Pay Bill in which the overtime is entered.

The Station Masters and Superintendents are responsible for seeing that the Staff do not work excessive hours.

GWR overtime allowance application form, Pilning, 1897

No 6019 *King Henry V*, working hard, passes Pilning High Level with the 8.00am Neyland to Paddington express, 10th February 1962.

Hugh Ballantyne

nature, leased a few acres and built a small brickworks at Cattybrook in 1865. A good investment, he supplied no less than 74,400,000 bricks for the Severn Tunnel. They were also used for building Fry's factory at Somerdale, Keynsham, the offices of the Imperial Tobacco Company at Bristol, and Portishead power station.

Before Pilning High Level on the main line, the Severn Beach branch curved off to the right to Pilning Low Level station opened in 1928 on the site of the original station, which had closed in 1886 with the withdrawal of the Portskewett to New Passage ferry on the opening of the Severn Tunnel. At the time of writing, just one train a day, Mondays to Fridays, in each direction calls at Pilning High Level, now simply Pilning. Pilning

High Level used to be important as goods trains were inspected before passing through the Severn Tunnel and special tunnel brake vans were added by gravitational shunting to heavier goods trains. Tunnel vans, unlike the normal GWR type, had closed, instead of open verandas, as being on an open variety was unpleasant when brakes needed to be applied or taken off and you were exposed to the choking fumes. Guards were specially rostered to work back and forth in these tunnel vans. The Severn Tunnel emergency train consisting of flat, tank (full of water for fire-fighting) and low wagons, is permanently stabled on the Up side. Until the opening of the Severn Bridge, cars were taken through the tunnel. The special train consisted of a single coach for passengers and as

2-6-2T No 6155 pilots an Up freight through Pilning High Level station on 12th November 1958. The White disc 'T5' identifies the banking engine supplied by Severn Tunnel Junction shed.

Author's Collection

No 4918 *Dartington Hall* has just emerged from the Severn Tunnel with the 12.50pm Cardiff to Brighton, 10th February 1962.

Hugh Ballantyne

many bogie flat wagons as were required for the number of cars to be carried. For safety, petrol had to be drained from the vehicles' fuel tanks, but the GWR replenished them at the other end with a quantity equal to that removed.

If a freight train needed assistance through the tunnel, a banker was coupled in front of the train engine and if help was still required beyond Pilning, the banker would be uncoupled and the train assisted from the rear. The reason for this manoeuvre was that exhaust from two engines toiling up the gradient through the single bore Patchway Tunnel would have created unacceptable conditions.

FERRY SERVICES

Sailings.—About every 20 minutes. 8 a.m. to 8 p.m.; additional, Thurs. and Sat., 9,10, 11. 11.30 p.m., winter time. Summer time, 7 a.m. to 10 p.m.; additional, Wed., Thurs., Sat., 1st June to 30 Sept., 10.30, 11, 11.30 p.m.

14 Dartmouth to Kingswear (Devonshire). Owners—Dartmouth Corporation. Lessees—General Estates Co., Ltd., The Lower Ferry, Kingswear. Phone—Kingswear 42. (Map 3.E.7.)
Charges.—(Including driver and passengers.) M/C., S. 6d.; R. 9d. Comb., S. 1s.; R. 1s. 6d. Car, S. 1s. 6d. to 2s. 6d. to 3s. 3d. Trailer Caravan, S. 2s.; R. 2s. 6d. Return tickets available for 1 month.
Sailings.—Continuous service throughout the year, viz.: Wkdays, 6 a.m. till 11 p.m., Suns., 8 a.m. till 11 p.m.

14a Dartmouth to Kingswear (Devonshire), The "Mew." Address—Great Western Railway, Kingswear. Telegraphic Address — Station-Master, Kingswear. (Map 3.E.7.)
Charges.—M/C., S. 6d.; R. 9d. Comb., S. 1s.; R. 1s. 6d. Car, S. 1s. 6d. to 2s. 6d.; R. 2s. to 3s. 3d. Above charges includes Motor and Trailer Caravans not carried. Return any time.
Sailings from Dartmouth.—Winter: Wkdays—Frequent sailings from 6.25 a.m. until 10.10 p.m. Sundays: 9.15 a.m. to 1.10 p.m., 4.20 p.m. to 10.15 p.m. Summer: Wkdays—6.25 a.m. to 11.5 p.m. Sundays, 9.15 a.m. to 2.15 p.m.; 4 p.m. to 10.15 p.m. Kingswear times, about ½ hour later.

15 Dartmouth Steam Ferry Bridge from Sandquay Point to Old Rock (Devonshire). Address—The Secretary, Messrs. Philip & Son. Ltd., Sandquay and Noss Engineering Works, Dartmouth. Phone — Dartmouth 6. Telegraphic Address—Philip, Dartmouth. (Map 3.E.7.)
Charges.—M/C., S. 6d.; R. 9d. Comb., S. 1s.; R. 1s. 6d. Car, S. 1s. 6d. to 2s. 6d.; R. 2s. to 3s. 3d., according to size. Caravan, as for cars. Trailer Caravan, S. 2s.; R. 2s. 6d. Passengers, 1d. Return tickets available for 1 month.
Sailings.—Wkdays: 1st April to 30th April, 7 a.m. to 8 p.m. 1st May to 31st May, 7 a.m. to 9 p.m. 1st June to 30th Sept., 7 a.m. to 10 p.m. 1st Oct. to 31st Oct., 7 a.m. to 9 p.m. 1st Nov. to 31st March, 7 a.m. to 7 p.m. Sun.: As above but commencing at 9 a.m.

16 Torpoint (Cornwall) to Devonport (Devonshire). Address—The Manager, Torpoint Ferry, Ferry Office, Torpoint. Phone—Torpoint 33. Telegraphic Address—Ferry, Torpoint. (Map 3.E.5.)
Charges.—M/C., 2d. Comb., 9d. Car, 1s. to 2s., according to size. Caravan, according to size. Trailer Caravan, S. 1s. Passengers, 1½d. each way.
Sailings.—Very frequent service from about 6.30 a.m. wkdays (Sun. 7 a.m.) to about 11.45 p.m..

17 Saltash (Cornwall) to St. Budeaux, Plymouth (Devonshire). Address—The Superintendent, Corporation Ferry Bridge, Saltash. Telegraphic Address —Ferry Superintendent, Saltash. (Map 3.E.5.)
Charges.—(Passengers included) M/C., S. 4d.; R. 6d. Comb., S. 8d.; R. 1s. Car, S. 1s. to 1s. 9d.; R. 2s. to 3s. 6d., according to size. Caravan (small) and Trailer Caravan, S. 1s. 6d.; R. 2s. Return tickets available for 14 days.
Sailings.—Very frequent service from about 6.45 a.m. to 11 p.m. (during Summer time, 6.15 a.m. to 11 p.m.). Sun., Gd. Fri. and Xmas Day, commences 7 a.m. then as for wkdays.

18 Fowey to Bodinnick (Cornwall). Address—Mr. William J. Green, Owner, The "Old Ferry" Inn, Bodinnick, Fowey, Cornwall. (Map 2.E.4.)
Charges.—M/C., 1s. Comb. or Tri-car, 2s. Car, 2s. 6d. Caravan, 3s. Car with trailer-caravan, 4s. Above include return same day.
Sailings.—As required from 7 a.m. till dark.

19 King Harry to Philleigh (Cornwall). Address—The Secretary, King Harry Steam Ferry Co., Ltd., Public Rooms, Truro. Telegraphic Address—Simmons Hodge, Truro. Phone—Truro 253. (Map 2 E.3.)
Charges.—M/C., S. 9d.; R. 1s. Comb., S. 8d.; R. 1s. Tri-car, R. 1s. 6d. Car, 2 seats, R. 3s.; 4 seats, R. 3s. 6d.; Car and trailer-caravan, R. 4s. Return available same day. Passengers, 3d.
Sailings.—Wkdays: ½ hourly between 7 a.m. and 7 p.m. (end March to end Sept., 8 p.m.). Sun.: From King Harry (Feock) side at 9.30 a.m. and 6.30 p.m. From Philleigh side at 9.45 a.m. and 6.65 p.m. Runs on bk. hols., Xmas Day, Good Friday.

20 Pilning Station (Gloucestershire) to Severn Tunnel Junction (Monmouthshire). Address—Superintendent of the Line, Great Western Railway, Paddington Station, London, W. Phones—Paddington 7000. Pilning Sta.—Pilning 6. Severn Tunnel Junction Sta.—Caldicot 10. Telegraphic Address—Traffic, Paddington, London. (Map 4.B.2.)
Charges (at Owner's risk).—M/C. (accompanied), 1s. 2d. to 1s. 11d., according to weight. Side-cars (accompanied), 1 seat, 1s. 6d.; 2 or more, 2s. 3d. Side-Cars must be detached or truck provided and charged as Motor-Cars. Cars (accompanied), up to 8 h.p., 5s.; over 8 h.p., 6s. Passengers, 3rd class, 1s. 11d. S.; 2s. 9d. return (monthly).
Service.—Cars are conveyed by certain trains booked to call at Severn Tunnel Junction and Pilning Stations.

508

FERRY SERVICES

Cars should be at the Station 10 minutes before the train is due to start. A previous advice should be sent to the Station by letter or telegram.

21 Beachley-Aust (Gloucestershire) Ferry. Address—Old Passage Severn Ferry Co., Ltd., The Pier, Beachley, Glos. Phones—Chepstow 412 or 268 (Residence), Pilning 19. (Map 4.B.2.)
Charges.—M/C., 1s. 6d. Comb. (driver included), 3s. Cars (driver included), under 8 h.p., S. 3s.; over 8 h.p., S. 4s. Caravan, 7s. 6d. Trailer Caravan, 4s. and 5s. Passengers, 1s.
Sailings.—Daily from 9 a.m. until dusk. Hourly service from either side. Motor-Cars cannot be carried at low water stages of High Spring Tides (see Time-Tables).

22 Neyland-Pembroke (Pembrokeshire). Address—F. R. Lee, Proprietor, Hobbs Point, Pembroke Dock. Phone—Pembroke Dock 32 and 36. (Map 10.F.2.)
Charges.—M/C., 3d. Comb., 6d. Cars, S. 1s. 6d. to 2s. 6d.; R. 2s. 6d. to 4s. Driver's fare included in above. Passengers, S. 4d.; R. 6d.
Sailings.—Wkdays: 6 a.m. to 9.30 p.m., every 20 mins. approx. Sun.: 7 a.m. to 9.30 p.m., every ½ hr. approx.

23 Liverpool (Lancashire) to Seacombe-Wallasey (Cheshire). Address—Ferries Manager, Seacombe Ferry, Wallasey, Cheshire. Phone—Wallasey 3671 and 3672. (Map 17.C.5.)
Charges.—Per Passenger Boats.—M/C., S. 6d. (Day). Comb., 8d. Per Luggage Boats—Tri-Car, 1s. Cars, according to size, 1s. to 2s. Trailer Caravan, 1s. to 2s. Passengers, 2d.
Sailings.—Passenger Service, wkdays and Sun. Luggage Service, wkdays only.—Punctual quarter-hourly service 6 a.m. to 8 p.m., and half-hourly to 10 p.m.

24 Birkenhead Corporation. Birkenhead (Woodside) (Cheshire) to Liverpool (Lancashire) per Passenger Steamers. Address—Birkenhead Corporation Ferries, Woodside, Birkenhead. Phone—Birkenhead 3080. Extensions 246, 247, 248, 249. Telegraphic Address—Ferries Manager, Woodside, Birkenhead. (Map 17.C.5.)
Charges.—(driver included). M/C., 6d. Comb., 9d. Passengers: Day Boats, 2d.; Night Boats, 3d.
Sailings.—Passenger Steamers. Frequent service day and night, wkdays and Sun.

24 (contd.) Birkenhead Corporation. Birkenhead (Woodside) (Cheshire) to Liverpool (Lancashire) per Goods and Vehicle Steamers. (See Passenger Service for other particulars.)
Charges.—Wkdays: (driver included) M/C., 6d. Comb., 9d. Car, 1s. to 2s., according to H.P. Caravan, as for Cars. Trailer Caravan, 1s. or 1s. 6d. Passengers, 2d.
Sailings.—Goods & Vehicle Steamers. From Liverpool, every 30 minutes from 6 a.m. to 10 p.m. From Birkenhead, every 30 minutes from 6.15 a.m to 9.45 p.m. Sailings on Bank Holidays as per special notices.
Motor Park, Woodside Ferry.—Open daily, 7.30 a.m. to 11.30 p.m. Closed on Sun., Gd. Fri. Xmas and Boxing Day. Charge, day (or part thereof), 1s.

24a The Mersey Tunnel.
Extract from Official Regulations.
Strict compliance with these regulations will help to ensure your safety, as well as that of others.
Speeds.
Slow Lane.—Minimum, 6 m.p.h. Maximum, 20 m.p.h.
Fast Lane.—Minimum, 20 m.p.h. Maximum, 35 m.p.h.
Keep in Lane.—OVERTAKING PROHIBITED.—NO CROSSING WHITE LINES EXCEPT AS INDICATED AT JUNCTIONS. KEEP 75 FEET APART. SOUNDING HORN PROHIBITED. HEADLIGHTS OUT IN TUNNEL. KEEP IN GEAR. COASTING PROHIBITED. OBSERVE AND OBEY TRAFFIC SIGNALS AND NOTICES.
Signal Lights.
Red—STOP. Amber—CAUTION. Green —PROCEED. GREEN ARROW at Liverpool Junction means filtration allowed to the left to New Quay exit.
If a "Stop Your Engine" signal is displayed, Stop Your Engine at Once, and keep it stopped until signal is extinguished and traffic is allowed to resume.
Petrol Reminder.
See that you have sufficient petrol in the tank. Vehicles requiring tyre or wheel changes, or breaking down or running out of fuel, will be removed to the most convenient exit by the Tunnel breakdown wagon. Any vehicle requiring to be so removed will be charged a fee equal to double its ordinary toll, in addition to the toll already paid.
Proceed through the Tunnel without stopping, unless prevented by traffic, traffic officers, traffic signals, or other unavoidable cause.
Maximum height of vehicle loaded, 13 ft. 6 in.; maximum width of vehicle loaded, 9 ft.; maximum weight of vehicle loaded, 10 tons per axle.
Charges (driver included) to be paid at toll booths, before entering tunnel.—M/C., 6d.; Comb., 9d.; Tri-car, 1s.; Cars, 1s. to 2s. Trailer, 1s. or 1s. 6d. Passengers, 2d.; under 14, 1d.
(See explanatory note at head of page 505.)

509

Details of GWR conveying cars through the Severn Tunnel – from AA Handbook, 1937–8

3. Bristol to Yate via Mangotsfield

The first proposal for a railway to run from Bristol in the direction of Yate was in 1803 when a horse tramway was planned to run from Coalpit Heath to the harbour at Bristol, but as its cost of £23,000 could not be raised, the scheme became abortive. In 1824 a railway was proposed to link Birmingham with Bristol for the purpose of taking goods to Bristol Docks. A partial survey was undertaken, but money and determination were lacking and the scheme fell into abeyance. The next proposal, the Bristol & Gloucestershire Railway was less ambitious, but succeeded. Authorised by Parliament on 19th June 1828, with a capital of £45,000, it was to run from Avon Street Wharf on the Floating Harbour, through St Philip's, Fishponds and Mangotsfield to collieries at Shortwood, Parkfield and Coalpit Heath. There was a lapse of time until subscriptions were completed, work not being begun until June 1829. The road was laid as a single track, but earthworks were prepared for double line. Funds ran out and an Extension of Time Act, 26th March 1834, allowed the railway three years to raise the extra £20,000 required.

The line opened on Thursday 6th August 1835 with the usual procession. A band was on one wagon and passengers were carried in closed cars. Each carriage had green baize-covered seats for 14 people. At the east end of Staple Hill Tunnel the procession was met by two carriages from Westerleigh with another band and more flags. They proceeded to Coalpit Heath where a feast was held. In the afternoon the procession returned, preceded by 50 wagons carrying a total of 200 tons of 'extra ordinary fine coal'. The single line had a gauge of 4 ft 8in. The rails were of fish-belly pattern held in iron chairs fixed to stone blocks. Although generally worked by horses and gravity, gradients being with the load practically all the way, letters have come to light suggesting that locomotives were used as well.

Lord Middleton, in a letter of 2nd February 1835 to Edward Francis Colston and forwarded to Sir John Smyth wrote: 'The Railway Company have determined on providing the Locomotive Power'. A few days later on 23rd February, Colston wrote to Sir John: 'I am sorry to learn that Bond and Winwood's Steam Carriage is blown to atoms, they must have been making some alterations in its construction to increase its velocity to two journeys per day . . . we must get some proper sized steam carriages on the Rail Road . . . steam generated in tubes and not in a boiler to render it more safe . . . charged 4½d per ton for Locomotive Power, 4d per ton Waggons.' This correspondence took place more than five months before the official opening.

Linked with the Bristol & Gloucestershire was the Avon & Gloucestershire Railway, a similar tramway built by the Kennet & Avon Canal. The AGR left the BGR at Mangotsfield and descended to the Avon at Keynsham.

Following the GWR acquiring an interest in the Bristol & Gloucestershire, a proposal was made to connect the BGR with the projected Cheltenham & Great Western Union Railway at Standish. There were fierce arguments and Parliament refused to sanction the extension in February 1837. The GWR offered its assistance and on 1st July 1839 an Act was obtained for this 22¼-mile extension and the name of the undertaking was shortened to the Bristol & Gloucester Railway. As Brunel was the engineer and the Great Western had subscribed £50,000 of the authorised capital of £400,000, the GWR considered the line a dependent. A depression in the iron trade allowed the BGR to purchase rails cheaply. These were of the bridge pattern and fastened to planking which was secured to longitudinal sleepers.

The gauge was not decided on at this time, but at the General Meeting held in Bristol on 31st March 1840 the Directors reported that it was 'essential to the interests of the undertaking that the line should be constructed on the same gauge as that of the Railway from Gloucester to Birmingham. On this line the narrow gauge has been adopted'. Construction to the standard gauge started the following year. Early in 1843 the BGR had second thoughts on the gauge question. The Cheltenham & Great Western Union Railway was about to be bought by the Great Western and the BGR felt it politic to be on good terms with them. It feared that unless the broad gauge was adopted, traffic for the west would be directed via Swindon, the GWR carrying the load all the way. Brunel probably encouraged them to adopt broad gauge. When the formal agreement was made with the GWR in April 1843, the BGR adopted broad gauge and was allowed to build a connection from Lawrence Hill so that it could use the GWR's Temple Meads station. In addition the BGR was allowed the use of GWR stations at Gloucester and Cheltenham.

Details of Goods Conveyance to and from Bristol, from an LMS book published in 1926

As terms for the BGR to be worked by the GWR could not be settled to the satisfaction of both sides, the BGR Directors arranged with Stothert, Slaughter & Company of Bristol to provide plant, and operated the line for the first ten years. Directors and their friends made a journey on 13th June 1844 from Bristol to Stonehouse hauled by *Bristol*. The line was opened ceremonially on 6th July, a free ride being offered to every BGR shareholder. The first train of 12 first and second class coaches holding nearly 550 passengers should have left Bristol at 10.00am, but was delayed until noon as the special from Gloucester carrying the Directors of the Birmingham & Gloucester Railway arrived late. The party returned to Bristol about 8.00pm. The line opened to the public on 8th July, six trains running daily in each direction, covering the distance of 37½ miles in 1½ hours. The passenger coaches were built by Williams, a Bristol coachmaker. They had iron frames and were sprung on Buchanan's patent new principle, considerably reducing noise and motion. The

Bath Chronicle reported: 'The carriages were remarkably easy and pleasant, and the oscillation, even at the highest speed, was very slight'. The first class coaches had three compartments with four seats each side; the second class coaches had four compartments each holding 12 passengers; third class coaches had standing accommodation only 'for the poorer class of travellers', open at the sides and having no roof. Within a week of the BGR's opening, three of the six stage coaches between Bristol and Gloucester stopped running.

The BGR carefully preserved the environment. Slopes beside the line were neatly covered with 'turfs of grass not less than 8 inches thickness with greensward outwards and well beat and pressed into place'. If the turf which had been kept was not considered good by the engineer, 8 inches of top soil had to be sown with ryegrass and clover seed mixed, no less than 14lbs of clover seed and one bushel of ryegrass per acre.

The Midland Railway made a better offer for the BGR than did the GWR and took the line on a perpetual lease from 1st July 1845, purchasing engines and plant for working the line from Stothert, Slaughter & Company. In 1848 four new engines were required. As the MR intended to convert the line to standard gauge in the not too distant future, Matthew Kirtley, the MR's Locomotive Superintendent ordered Sharp Brothers to make them convertible. They complied by building standard gauge engines with long axles, the wheels being outside the axleboxes. Starting work on the broad gauge in 1848–9, when standard gauge was laid in 1854 they were sent to Derby, the axles shortened and the wheels placed within the double frames. They had the honour of being the first British convertible engines to be built. Standard gauge working began on 22nd May 1854, some of the redundant broad gauge engines being sold to the North Devon Railway, and coaches to the Bristol & Exeter. The broad gauge metals had to be kept in situ because of the B&E coal train which ran daily to and from Parkfield colliery until 1882 to avoid transhipment at Bristol.

As the former GWR and MR each had a line between Bristol and Westerleigh, an economy measure was planned so that on 3rd January 1970 the former route should be closed, trains travelling via Filton instead of Mangotsfield, but as a 40-ft section of the 20-ft high embankment at Fishponds slipped on 26th December 1969, the line was actually closed on this date. The section from Mangotsfield North Junction to Yate was kept open to give access to the Mangotsfield to Bath branch until this closed on 31st May 1971. The line from Yate now ends at Avon County Council's Westerleigh Refuse Terminal, first used on 19th November 1985. This stretch of line is currently used also for training track machine operators.

During World War Two, Parnall's workers used Yate station. An airfield had been built in 1916–7 to provide flight test and delivery facilities for No 3 (Western) Aircraft Repair Depot. Abandoned after WW1, George Parnall & Company took over the buildings in 1925. Ten years later a new undertaking was set up, Parnall Aircraft Limited, which also built Fraser-Nash aircraft gun-turrets. In addition to this work, the firm became the largest sub-contractor of Spitfire components in the country.

Description of the line from Bristol to Yate

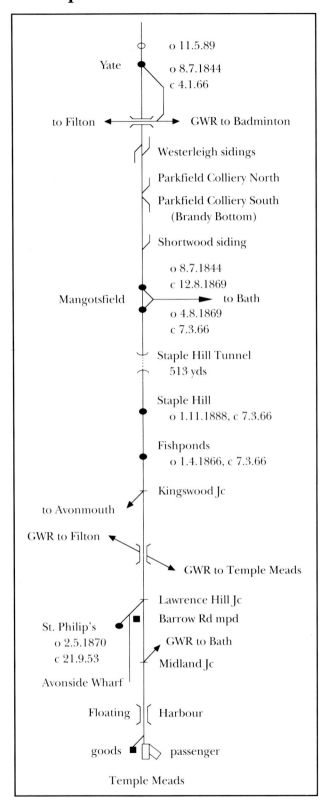

Diagrammatic map of the MR/LMS route from Bristol Temple Meads to Yate

In steam days passenger trains for Yate usually left from Brunel's train shed at Temple Meads, curving northwards from the Bath line by Bristol East box. Not far beyond was Barrow Road shed, the MR's Bristol motive power depot, built for £20,000 in 1871 on the site of the BGR's shed. It received improvements in 1938–9 when mechanical coal and ash-handling plants were constructed, coal wagons being moved to the former by capstan. On one occasion a wagon believed to be filled with coal was not checked and was actually loaded with clay pipes. These were tipped into the large coal hopper and then staff were faced with the problem of getting them out. Barrow Road was the last steam shed in Bristol, closing on 14th October 1965. Its site is now covered by Avon County Council's Great Western Refuse Transfer Station where rubbish is compacted and placed in closed containers to be carried away by rail.

Next to the motive power depot was the MR carriage shed, cattle dock, goods shed and yard together with St Philip's passenger station. The goods station and yard covering nearly six acres was completed in July 1866, having taken two years to construct. Inside the goods shed, measuring 180 ft by 133 ft, were 15 hydraulic cranes of Sir William Armstrong's patent, so placed on the platform that as one lifted goods from trucks on to the platform, another lifted goods from the platform to wagons on the other side. Wagons were moved to different roads by hydraulically-powered traversing tables and similarly-driven capstans capable of pulling 80 tons, so preventing

TRANSFER TRAINS BETWEEN PYLLE HILL AND MIDLAND YARD, BRISTOL.									
		WEEK DAYS ONLY.							
STATIONS.		1	2	3	4	5			
		B.G. Goods	N.G. Mid. Goods	B.G. Goods	N.G. Mid. Engine Wagons	N.G. Mid. Engine Wagons			
		A.M.	A.M.	P.M.	P.M.	P.M.			
Bristol (Pylle Hill)	dep.	8 15	9 55	5 0	7 0	11 40	....	...	....
Midland	arr.	8 30	10 10	5 15	7 15	11 55	..	..	..

		WEEK DAYS ONLY.							
STATIONS.		1	2	3	4	5			
		N.G. Mid. Goods	B.G. Goods	N.G. Mid. Goods	B.G. Goods	N.G. Mid. Goods			
		A.M.	NOON	P.M.	P.M.	P.M.			
Midland	dep.	9 25	12 0	6 5	6 30	11 10	....	...	....
Bristol (Pylle Hill)	arr.	9 40	12 15	6 20	6 45	11 25	..	..	..

Timetable for the transfer between Pylle Hill and Midland Yard, October 1886

LMS 0-6-0T No 1874 in the yard of Barrow Road locomotive shed, September 1947. Barrow Road Bridge is on the far right, two point levers in the foreground.
Roger Venning

Class 3MT 2-6-2T No 82004 passes Barrow Road mpd with a Temple Meads to Bath and Bournemouth West train on 26th September 1964. No 4919 *Donnington Hall* stands left.
R E Toop

2-6-2T No 41240 leaves St Philip's, c1952, with a train to Bath Green Park. The goods yard is to the left. *Lens of Sutton*

the shed's interior from being polluted by locomotive smoke. The hydraulic power came from Armstrong's patent accumulator worked by two engines of about 60 hp. Below the shed was spacious cellarage capable of storing over 15,000 hogsheads. Stabling was provided for 50 MR horses. The 20-road goods yard closed on 1st April 1967. At St Philip's the LMS had a gas plant for recharging gas-lit coaches and cooking facilities in restaurant cars. As an economy measure the gas works were closed in 1934, supplies then being purchased from the GWR, saving the LMS £350 a year.

St Philip's passenger station was opened on 2nd May 1870 for Bristol to Bath local traffic to ease the congestion at Temple Meads. It was a terminal station with but one platform, covered by a ridge and furrow glass roof. It closed from 21st September 1953, all passenger trains reverting to Temple Meads. In order to work empty coaches to Temple Meads, a Midland engine had to draw coaches from St Philip's carriage sidings to Lawrence Hill Junction, and then back the whole train, maybe 12 coaches in length, to Temple Meads old station, a highly unsatisfactory working, having to travel about a mile in reverse, when pushing such a long train round curves and over such busy junctions.

From St Philip's to Mangotsfield the former track formation is today followed by the Bristol & Bath Railway Path. From Lawrence Hill Junction, trains climbed at 1 in 69/70 for two miles to Fishponds, quite a few requiring a banking engine. Just north of Lawrence Hill Junction a wagon works could be seen on the left and shortly beyond, the MR crossed the GWR line to Filton. Following closure of the Lawrence Hill to Mangotsfield line on 26th December 1969, a new spur was built linking a siding of the former GWR's Lawrence Hill goods yard with the former Midland's main line in order

WEEKDAYS.

CLASSIFICATION	Engine and Brake to Avonmouth	Engine and Brake		Light Engine	Light Engine	Light Engine		To Water Orton.	Light Engine to Bristol	Empties from West Depot, 9.15 a.m.	Light Engine	Engine and Brake, 9.30 a.m. from Avonmouth	Railsworths arr. 10.43, dep. 10.49		10.20 a.m. Engine and Brake from Stapleton Rd.	Empties to Washwood Heath	Engine and Brake, Goods Shed.			Empties from Clifton Down, 10.40 a.m.
Target No...	44	44	12	35	35	35				31	38	43	38	33	44		14	14	11	14	34
	G	G	K	G	G	G		F	G	K	G	H	K	K	G	J	F	G	J	K	J
	Q a.m.	a.m. 8 23	a.m.	SX 8 50	SO 8 50	SX 8 50		SX 8 50		a.m.	a.m.	a.m.	a.m.	a.m.	a.m.	a.m. 10 40	a.m.	p.m. SO	p.m. SO	p.m. SX	a.m.
BRISTOL (St.Phillips) dep.																					
Engine Shed Sidings	8 12	8 25		8 53	8 53	8 53		8 53		9 37	9 55					10 44	10 45				11 15
Lawrence Hill Junc.	8 17																				11 18
Kingswood Junc.												9 23			10 30	10 55					
Fish Ponds ...... arr.		8 33		9 3	9 3	9 3		9 3		9 44		9 55		10 25	10 35	11 3	11 13				11 26
dep.																					
BATH (Mid.Bge.Rd.) dep.																					
Weston																11 10			12 10		11 35
Bitton					9			9							10 42	11 15	11 40				11 40
Warmley ...... arr.		8 40		9 10	9 10	9 10		9 10		9 48	10 6	10 11		10 41	10 49						
dep.																					
Mangotsfield South Jc.		8 45		9 16	9 16	9 16		9 16		9 55		10 18	10 40	10 45	10 52		11 49				
Mangotsfield Station Jc.		8 48		9 20	9 20	9 20		9 20		9 50		10 22	10 56								
Mangotsfield North Jc.								9 55													
Westerleigh South Junc.								10 0			10 12										
WESTERLEIGH											10 18										
SIDINGS ...... dep.															11 12				12 18	12 38	
Westerleigh North Junc.					10 52																
Yate South Junc.																				12 43	
Yate ...... arr.													11 29					12 21	12 39	2 0	
dep.																					
Wickwar ...... arr.			10 30																		
Charfield			10 43										11 39					12 25	12 45	2 5	
Berkeley Road S. Junc.																					
Berkeley Road ...... dep.			10 50																		
Coaley Junc. ...... dep.			10 55																		
Frocester			12 0										11 58								
Stonehouse (Bristol Road) dep.			12 5																		
Standish Junc. ...... dep.																					
Hempstead Sids. ...... dep.																					
Tuffley Junc. ...... dep.																					
High Orchard ...... dep.																					
Barton Street Junc.														12 14							
GLOUCESTER (Eastgate) ...... arr.														12 17							
BARNWOOD SIDS. ...... arr.																					

Working timetable for freight trains from Bristol to Gloucester, 1953

The attractive brick-built station at Fishponds, 21st April 1960, looking north.

Author

Great Western Refuse Transfer Station at Barrow Road, looking towards Avon Wharf, 17th March 1990. Travelling cranes lift refuse containers over the fence from yard to train.   *Author*

to give access to Avon Wharf. This new chord line opened on 1st February 1970, but at the time of writing is about to be closed south of ACC's Great Western Refuse Transfer Station as its cement traffic will be concentrated at Lawrence Hill. At Kingswood Junction a line, closed on 14th June 1965, led in from Avonmouth and Stapleton Road gas works, while on the opposite side a line served Kingswood Colliery.

Fishponds station opened in 1866 as Stapleton, being renamed on 1st July 1867. It had three platforms, one being a bay for Clifton Down trains. On 1st July 1885, a Travelling Post Office pick-up apparatus was fixed beside the Up line. This station, like Staple Hill and Mangotsfield, closed when passenger traffic on the Bath branch was withdrawn on 7th March 1966. The extensive goods yard at Fishponds was closed three months before. From the station a siding led to Avonside Engine Works. The main line climbed a gradient of 1 in 583 to Staple Hill. Situated in a cutting, it had timber buildings. At one time Staple Hill was well-used by commuters because in days when people had to think about every penny, although

electric trams were more accessible, they were more expensive than a railway season ticket.

The line became level and entered the 513-yd long Staple Hill Tunnel, the portal having a facing of rough large stones. Originally 12 ft wide, the tunnel's width was increased to 26 ft by the BGR

Railwaymen were very keen on First Aid. Fishponds station St John's Ambulance team, which won the Bristol Championships in 1904, pose for this picture.   *M J Tozer Collection*

Mangotsfield station on 22nd April 1954: Gloucester lines left, Bath right.

Dr A J G Dickens

widening it on the north side. The two rectangular shafts used in its excavation were left open for light and because of its original single line construction, the shafts were over what became the Down line. At the far end of the tunnel is a deep cutting and the line fell at 1 in 993 to Mangotsfield.

Mangotsfield station was situated at the west junction of a triangle where the Gloucester line curved sharply north, and the Bath branch sharply south. The original station was at the North Junction, but closed when the newer station opened with the branch to Bath. On the north side of the station was a steep rock face and on the south a wooden hoarding to shield the platforms from the wind. There were six platforms, but latterly only four were regularly used by passenger trains; the other roads 'under the rock' and 'behind the box' being little used. Mangotsfield was principally a junction station used by passengers changing trains, although used also to a certain extent by employees of Carson's chocolate factory. Many racing pigeons were liberated from the station. Mangotsfield North Junction was originally the junction of the Avon & Gloucestershire and Bristol & Gloucestershire

Railways and latterly the junction with the Bath branch. The former station house still stands.

To the north, the main line had sidings serving various industries – Shortwood Brick Works, Brandy Bottom Colliery, South Pit, Parkfield Colliery – all the colliery sidings being closed by 1940. On the Down side, north of Shortwood Bridge, within living memory coal seams opened up when permanent way men were clearing the bank. No doubt several men took some home to burn. Further north was Westerleigh Marshalling Yard. Opened in 1900–1 to ease congestion at Bath and Bristol, it consisted of 13 Up and 12 Down roads. Closed in 1965, part of the site was re-developed 20 years later as Avon County Council's Westerleigh Refuse Terminal, while at the time of writing an oil terminal is being built on another part of the site for Murco Petroleum where two new sidings will be laid. It is anticipated that the terminal will be commissioned in the spring of 1991 when one or two trains will arrive daily. During WW2 the yard was 'protected' by dummy wooden guns ostensibly designed to give a frightening impression from the air but in reality only giving reassurance to the civilian population. From Westerleigh Yard, a mile-long branch led to

Ex-Somerset & Dorset Railway 2-8-0 No 53808 passes Staple Hill station, c1960. *Author's Collection*

An Up goods and the 3.05pm Paddington to Temple Meads express cross the ex-Midland line at Westerleigh, 21st April 1960.

Author

Girls from Carson's Chocolate Factory bidding farewell at Mangotsfield to WW1 troops from the Beaufort War Hospital at Fishponds. The soldiers had been entertained at Carson's.

Downend Local History Society

Brunel-designed buildings at Yate, looking north, 11th May 1961. Notice the elegant footbridge. *Author*

Coalpit Heath, the last colliery closing in 1950. Part of the line was retained until 1956 for wagon storage. The Coalpit Heath line had its own locomotives, one, *Lord Salisbury*, ending its days at Norton Hill Colliery, Midsomer Norton. The main line passed under the Bristol Parkway to Swindon line and under the line from the GWR's Westerleigh Junction.

The original Yate station, sketched either by I K Brunel himself or a member of his staff, was a pleasing design in brick relieved with stone, the main offices being on the Bristol platform. Opposite was a delightful waiting shelter in pavilion style. Both had large flat canopies for protecting passengers from the weather. As the awnings had no slope to enable the rain water to

Yate: arrival of the first service train at the new station, the 6.52am Gloucester to Temple Meads on 15th May 1989, worked by unit No 150.247. *Author*

Plaque at Yate station. *Author*

drain off, they were weather-proofed with a sheet of lead fixed to the canopy with flat-sided, round-topped battens over which the lead was rolled. This resulted in a decorative, shiny, ribbed surface. The goods station which still stands, was situated in a very cramped position between the Down platform and the road overbridge. To make the utmost use of the space, short sidings radiated from a wagon turntable. A TPO apparatus was installed in 1898.

Increasing competition from road transport caused a decline in traffic and it closed to passengers in 1965 and to goods the following year, but it was a different story 24 years later when road traffic had developed to such an extent that using roads caused problems and rail travel looked so much more inviting. Yate station was rebuilt, the Down platform on a site slightly to the north of the old one and officially re-opened on 11the May 1989 and to the public four days later. Officials say that traffic from the new station is 'more than anticipated'.

4. Filton to Avonmouth

Following the growth of Avonmouth Docks, the GWR decided that it would improve access by building an alternative to the steeply-graded line through Clifton Down Tunnel. When the Bristol & South Wales Direct Railway was opened in 1903 this need became pressing and so a line was planned from Filton through Henbury. Messrs Lovatt, the contractors, began work on 13th May 1907. On 9th May 1910, the 6¾-mile long line was opened providing a new outlet for up country traffic. As well as being useful for goods traffic, this line provided rail communication for the expanding suburbs of Bristol. The single line was doubled in stages, work being completed by May 1917 to cope with wartime traffic to and from Avonmouth and the factories en route. During WW1, plans were drawn up for constructing a curve from Filton West Junction to Patchway and earthworks were made, but no track laid, this having to wait until 22nd February 1971. The branch had been closed to regular passenger traffic from 23rd November 1964 and subsequently singled, excursions continuing to run to Clifton Down for Bristol Zoo and it was in fact especially for these 'Monkey Specials' from South Wales that the new curve was laid. Lately, 'Monkey Specials' have become rare, only one or two a year being run.

Description of the line from Filton to Avonmouth

The first station, Filton (Gloucester Road) Halt, has an interesting history. Closed in 1915 as a wartime economy measure, it reopened as North Filton Platform in 1926. Although closed to the public in 1964 it remained open for unadvertised workmen's services until 9th May 1986. A short distance west is an interesting and unusual level crossing. After WW2, the Bristol Aeroplane Company at Filton developed the large Brabazon airliner and between 13th October and 10th November 1947, temporary single line working was instituted between Henbury and Filton West. This allowed the installation of an aircraft level crossing over the railway which gave a taxi-track from the building hangar to a new runway allowing the aircraft to take off. When BAC wished to take aircraft over the crossing they rang Filton West signalbox and, if the line was clear, a release was given to the motors operating the sliding gates. After the passage of an aircraft, BAC restored the gates to normal and, providing a proving circuit was made, normal train operation continued. Today the telephone is connected to the Bristol MAS box and tested daily. The crossing is used intermittently, usually several times a week and sometimes several times a day.

Power-operated gates at the BAC crossing, Filton, 21st August 1980. *Author*

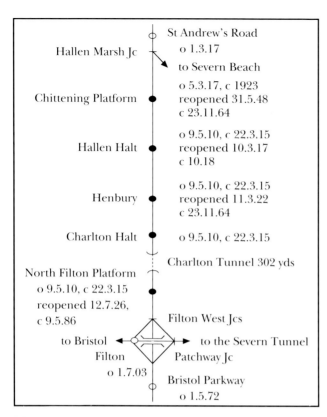

St Andrew's Road
o 1.3.17

Hallen Marsh Jc

to Severn Beach

Chittening Platform
o 5.3.17, c 1923
reopened 31.5.48
c 23.11.64

Hallen Halt
o 9.5.10, c 22.3.15
reopened 10.3.17
c 10.18

Henbury
o 9.5.10, c 22.3.15
reopened 11.3.22
c 23.11.64

Charlton Halt
o 9.5.10, c 22.3.15

Charlton Tunnel 302 yds

North Filton Platform
o 9.5.10, c 22.3.15
reopened 12.7.26,
c 9.5.86

Filton West Jcs

to Bristol

to the Severn Tunnel

Filton
o 1.7.03

Patchway Jc

Bristol Parkway
o 1.5.72

Diagrammatic map of the route from Filton to St Andrew's Road

The main engineering feature on the line is the 302-yd long Charlton Tunnel. Beyond was Charlton Halt, closed in 1915. Henbury was the principal station on the line and built in the usual red brick Great Western architecture of the period. An unusual feature was a goldfish pond on its platforms. Although closed to the public from 1915 to 1922, it was still served by an unadvertised workmen's service, a maximum of 6,600 travelling daily. From 2nd April 1917, permits were issued instead of tickets, their cost being charged to the Ministry of Munitions. Hallen Halt also enjoyed a chequered history. Closed with other stations on the line in 1915, it was reopened from 1917 to 1918 for workers of a nearby war supplies factory. Chittening Platform was built during WW1 to serve what would have been the second largest government factory in the country. Opened for workmen in 1917, it closed in 1923, being re-opened with an austere corrugated asbestos shelter on 27th October 1941 to workmen, and to the public in 1948. The line trails in to the Severn Beach branch at Hallen Marsh Junction. St Andrew's Road, originally opened during WW1 as a workmen's platform, remains a rather bleak station in an industrial area.

The attractive, neat, brick-built station at Henbury on 31st October 1958, looking towards Avonmouth.   *Author*

5. Hotwells to Severn Beach

Towards the middle of the last century, some ships were of such size that they had too great a draught to navigate the Avon successfully to Bristol, matters being brought to a head on 10th November 1851 when the 3,000 ton paddle steamer *Demarara* built at Bristol, was being towed to Glasgow for her engines to be fitted. Proceeding downstream, her bows struck the right-hand bank while the strongly ebbing tide swung her stern round to the left bank causing her back to break as she settled down. This episode made some shipowners afraid to use Bristol in case their vessels foundered in a similar manner. To avoid this difficulty, back in 1845 Brunel had conceived a floating pier at Portbury, but this scheme fell a victim of the depression in the Railway Mania, and the company formed was wound up in 1851. Ten years later, the Bristol Port Railway & Pier announced its intention of building a line from a terminus at Hotwells for 5¾ miles to Avonmouth where it was to end at a deep water pier. The line was to follow the river closely, the first mile or so

running at the foot of the Avon Gorge. Since it was not proposed to cater for anything but purely local traffic, no connection with other railways in Bristol was considered necessary. The pier was to be suitable for landing passengers, livestock and merchandise. Large vessels could partly unload and then proceed to Bristol instead of having to wait at Kingroad eight or ten days for a favourable tide.

The scheme received Royal Assent on 17th June 1862 and the first sod was turned at Shirehampton on 19th February 1863 by Mrs Sholto Vere Hare, Mayoress of Bristol. With the aid of a polished oak spade, she placed the sod on which reposed a bouquet of violets and primroses into a polished oak wheelbarrow. The contractors were Messrs Waring Brothers who also maintained and worked the railway on its completion. The line was standard gauge, but the sleepers were such that broad gauge could have been adopted without much expense or delay.

As the arrangements were incomplete, the Directors withheld the precise date of opening

Permanent way men on the Bristol Port Railway & Pier, c1900.

Author's Collection

93

(6th March 1865) so that their limited resources would not be overstretched and the public receive a poor first impression. Timetables were posted outside Clifton station just a few minutes before the first train left and a short paragraph appeared in the *Bristol Times & Mirror*. In the evening of the opening day the contractors treated their employees to a dinner.

On 27th April, the 'commodious landing stage' was brought up channel from Cardiff to Avonmouth and moved to its permanent place. Early on 24th May, Waring commenced the operation of fixing pontoons and floating bridges and completed the task early the next day. The General Steam Navigation Company's *SS Apollo* was the first vessel to use the pier when she landed her cabin passengers and luggage at 10.00am on Saturday 3rd June 1865, having left Cork at 4.00pm the previous afternoon. Passengers travelled to Bristol by the Bristol Port Railway & Pier and were able to catch the 12.15pm from Temple Meads to Paddington, arriving there at 3.00pm having covered the whole journey from Cork in 23 hours, thereby saving at least four hours by landing at Avonmouth. Unfortunately for the company, the deep water channel quickly silted up and by 1871 only eight feet of water remained. At first the railway only possessed one locomotive, purchasing a second later. Six passenger trains ran in each direction and on Sundays there were four Down and five Up, with a time allowance of 30 minutes for the 5¾ miles. The 20 passenger coaches were painted in yellow and white livery. Goods wagons – the company owned six – were attached to the rear of passenger trains as required. Ordinary running repairs were carried out at the company's Shirehampton headquarters, but when a more extensive overhaul was required, the engines had to be sent away and sometimes had to wait until the company could save sufficient funds to have the work carried out. Both engines were overhauled at different times by Peckett's. When either was under repair, a replacement was hired from the Midland Railway. As there was no rail connection, it had to be transported on a horse-drawn lorry. On one occasion as the lorry was proceeding along the newly-made Perry Road one Whit Saturday, it became embedded in soft ground and 60 horses were required to pull it out. Eventually it arrived at the rail-head in time to work the holiday traffic.

To encourage traffic to use the railway, a separate venture was started, the Avonmouth Hotel Company, which opened a leisure complex consisting of an hotel, concert hall and pleasure garden on Easter Monday 10th April 1865. It adjoined the range of the 1st Gloucestershire Rifle Volunteer Corps which used the line when travelling to and from practice. The range was also used by Clifton College Volunteers. Unfortunately on 16th February 1878, a sixth former returning by rail from practice accidentally discharged a rifle, the shot killing a master in the compartment.

On Whit Monday and Tuesday 1865, the 1st Gloucestershire's band performed in the hotel garden while Mr Matthews' quadrille band played in the concert hall. Archery, quoits, croquet, Aunt Sally and other amusements in the hotel grounds succeeded in attracting thousands of passengers down the railway to Avonmouth and tea and shrimps at the hotel became a popular half-holiday outing. It was originally envisaged that the hotel and grounds would attract 100,000 visitors annually, each entrant paying threepence, but although the enterprise enjoyed an initial popularity, it was financially disastrous. In 1873 the hotel's expenditure for the first half of the year was £252 and income only £180, the balance sheet showing a cumulative deficit of £2,922.

The BPRP did not wish to remain detached, but sought to be connected with other lines and as early as 1866 a survey was carried out for the construction of an underground line from its Hotwells terminus to Temple Meads. In the event the link was via the Clifton Extension Railway from just north of Stapleton Road station to Sneyd Park, involving a tunnel through Clifton Down. The tunnel was cut with the aid of a diamond boring machine and its inventor, Major Beaumont MP, descended the shaft at the end of Pembroke Road on 11th July 1872 to see his machine at work. Cutting facets of black diamonds were fixed round the end of a steel tube to form a kind of auger. This tube was revolved rapidly by compressed air and advanced so that its diamond points came into contact with the rock. Water forced through the tube washed away grit and kept the tube cool. A smooth-surfaced core was cut out by this drill and then a blasting charge inserted.

Boring the tunnel proved aggravating to people living nearby and in July 1872 a petition was presented to the GWR and MR by residents of Durdham Down complaining of dense opaque smoke from engine chimneys 'which frequently occasions the most serious nuisance and annoyance combined with the noise of blasting'. George Ashmead, surveyor to the extension and also the BPRP's arbitrator, mentioned an explosion in the tunnel works under the Down

Staff at Redland station with 'CER' (Clifton Extension Railway) in script on their caps. The ticket collector stands in the centre.

M J Tozer Collection

and feared a repetition would prevent people coming forward to rent houses owned by the company above the line of the tunnel works. A tenant in one of the company's houses in Hampton Park adjoining the railway was forced to leave by the annoyance and danger from the continual blasting from the railway, and the company paid him £30 compensation for the expense of removal; while John Carr, tenant of Hooks Mills, was granted £100 for loss of water supply. The following May his stream was still blocked by fallen stones and rubbish from the embankment.

On 1st October 1874, the 1½ miles of line from Narroways Hill Junction to Clifton Down was opened. The intermediate station at Montpelier boasted of separate ticket windows for the GWR and MR. Clifton Down Tunnel was finished on 12th February 1875, but the Board of Trade would not allow it to be opened because of a defect in the track and signalling at Sneyd Park Junction. Freight trains were allowed to use it from 24th February 1877, the day the dock was opened at Avonmouth. Eventually passenger trains started

running through Clifton Down to Avonmouth on 1st September 1885, the GWR providing a service from Temple Meads, and the MR from its terminus at St Philip's. The following year the Midland withdrew its service, but still continued to work from Mangotsfield to Clifton Down, an operation started when the extension was opened. This service was withdrawn on 31st March 1941.

Meanwhile, the Bristol Port Railway & Pier had run into financial difficulties and was taken over jointly by the GWR and MR on 1st September 1890. At the last minute these two companies decided to employ all the BPRP's servants and on 30th August, drivers and firemen who had been doubtful about their future, received the good news that they could continue in their situations. The *Bristol Times & Mirror* reported the GWR's disastrous start when it woefully underestimated the requirements of the daily traffic and came unstuck with the 7.15am, the very first train.

Presumably with a view to taking this train to Avonmouth, there was hooked on to it a dandy little steam kettle that Tommy All Hot, the baked potato man, might well have been proud of. As a strictly necessary consequence, the gay procession of smartly upholstered and newly-painted carriages, headed by their toy engine, came to a dead stand in attempting to mount the incline at Horseshoe Point and there remained in undignified inertness until the additional engine could be obtained from Sneyd Park Junction to second the efforts of the puny puffer in front. We are informed that the exclamations of the most forcible character rang out on the morning air in lusty chorus from the 468 working men passengers who were subject to this delay, which was so great that the 8.30am train from Hotwells and the 9.00am from Avonmouth had to be dropped out of the time bill altogether.

With the development of Avonmouth Docks and road transport, the route taken by the road over the Downs with a ruling gradient of 1 in 11 was unsatisfactory. As the width of the Avon Gorge allowed insufficient room for both road and railway, it was decided that the line would be closed and replaced by an inter-urban tramway mainly running on its own right of way. The road construction costs of the Portway were estimated at £401,000 with an additional £328,000 for 4 miles 7 chains of tramway, though in the event, the rapid transport scheme was abandoned in favour of more versatile buses. Bristol Corporation took

over the railway from Hotwells to Sneyd Park Junction by an Act of 16th August 1920. Hotwells station closed on 19th September 1921 when trains terminated at Hotwells Extension Platform at the west end of No 2 tunnel, and this too was finally closed on 3rd July 1922.

As an economy measure the line between Narroways Hill Junction and Avonmouth was singled on 19th October 1970, the double track through Clifton Down station being left as a passing loop.

To improve access to and from Avonmouth, a line was built to Pilning mainly along the bank of the Severn. Opened to goods on 5th February 1900, it was adapted for passenger traffic, excursion trains using a platform at Severn Beach at the Whit weekend, 5th June 1922, and opening for a regular summer service from Bristol on 10th July and again the following year. These trials proving successful, a permanent station was built in 1923. Unusual in design, its platform was uncluttered by buildings or even a canopy, but the brick-constructed buildings at right angles to the branch had a covered waiting area. An all-the-year-round service started on 26th May 1924 and was extended to Pilning on 23 June 1928. An attempt was made in the summer of 1938 to popularise Severn Beach and for the first time through excursions ran from Redditch, Great Malvern, Birmingham and Gloucester via Clifton Down and Avonmouth Dock, LMS engines working as far as the latter station.

Exchange of single line tablets at Severn Beach signalbox with reflection of the box in the window of a dmu. 3rd June 1963.   *Author*

Description of the line from Bristol to Avonmouth

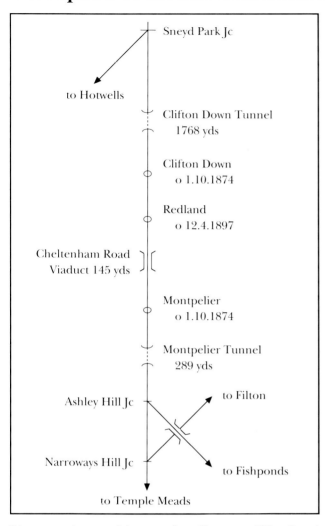

Diagrammatic map of the route from Narroways Hill to Sneyd Park Junction

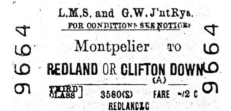

The main feature of the 1¾-mile long connection between the MR at Kingswood Junction and the Clifton Extension Railway at Ashley Hill Junction was a 405-ft long, 7-arch viaduct over Coombe Brook and a 681-ft long viaduct over the River Frome, the tallest of the 13 arches being 65 ft high. It was blown up on 26th May 1968, the site being required for part of the M32. The line had been shut on 14th June 1965 following the closure of Westerleigh Yard, as latterly the line had been used principally by Avonmouth to Westerleigh freights. The 1 in 76 rise from Narroways Hill Junction continued through the 289-yd long Montpelier Tunnel with its utilitarian brick eastern mouth and more imposing stone west portal, the exit being directly into Montpelier station. The tunnel was most useful to one regular traveller who used to doze from Temple Meads; the change of sound in the tunnel woke him ready to alight at the station. Situated on a sharp curve, Montpelier was in the domestic style of architecture and built of pennant stone with freestone dressings and coigns of yellow stone obtained from a cutting at Whiteladies Road. In February 1888, the Joint Committee ordered that the name on the station nameboards should be painted with one 'L' instead of two. Luggage traffic was heavy at the end of the week for incoming, and at the beginning of the week for outgoing. This was because at the beginning of the century, 200 to 300 commercial travellers used the station and required their samples to be stored, reclaiming them on Monday. Nearly £1 was collected in fees each Monday, and most articles were only charged a penny. Many commercial travellers had an excess weight of baggage on trains from Montpelier and if asked to pay an excess, threatened to direct all possible traffic from the Great Western. On 18th February 1907, 22 travellers were excessed a total of £2.6.7d.

Beyond the station, the line crosses the 2-arch Cheltenham Road Viaduct, consisting of a girder bridge made by Smedley Brothers of Belper in 1873, plus five more arches beyond. The gradient, which had eased to 1 in 400 through the station, now steepens to 1 in 76 and then eases to 1 in 160 crossing Redland Road. 550 passengers booked from Redland station on its opening day, but a contemporary writer believed that none of these were new passengers, but were those who would otherwise have booked from Clifton Down or Montpelier. Rather oddly the ticket office was a

2-6-2T No 5532 enters Clifton Down with an Up train. Notice the attractive roof canopy and its supports. Probably the cars parked to the right of the station drive belong to commuters.
M E J Deane

Ventilating shaft of Clifton Down Tunnel at the top of Upper Belgrave Road, 28th September 1974. *Author*

West portal of Clifton Down Tunnel from the cab of a dmu with permanent way men's hut on right. 14th June 1988. *Author*

separate building at the bottom of the incline at Lovers' Walk.

The line becomes level just before Clifton Down station which has two 500-ft long platforms, each formerly spanned by an 'A' type roof with fluted glass. The building, in modified Gothic style, cost £20,000. In its heyday it had a superb mansion-like booking hall with a huge fireplace at each end. Outside was a commodious carriage drive. The goods yard dealt with heavy coal traffic. Shops have been built above the station, some customers travelling by rail to use the facilities.

The line falls at 1 in 64 beyond the station through a 1,768-yd long tunnel at a maximum depth of 160 ft below ground level. The bore is straight and it is possible to see all the way through. In steam days this was often far from being the case; smoke hung round the Clifton Down exit, obscuring it, with the consequent risk of Up trains over-running the platform, so in October 1924 a clapper and gong were installed,

operated by the wheels of passing trains. Sited 100 yds from the upper mouth, it enabled drivers to check their position audibly. To improve the ventilation provided by the two vertical shafts, in 1950 an old shaft leading out to the face of the gorge was re-opened after having been blocked for many years. Originally it had been used as a stable for ponies employed in tunnel construction. A ganger's cabin was hewn out of the side of the tunnel on the Down side, approximately midway. The rising gradient caused problems to freight trains, it being essential to have a boiler full of steam and a box full of fire. In the event of a train stalling in the tunnel, the train was divided and taken to Clifton Down in two portions, the guard going back to the mouth of the tunnel to protect his train. The Clifton Extension joined the Bristol Port Railway at Sneyd Park Junction.

The BPRP Hotwells station was situated in the picturesque Avon Gorge, almost immediately below the suspension bridge. To save space in a rather congested location between the foot of the cliff and the river, a turntable connected the platform road with the run-round loop, though this interesting feature was removed in 1893 when the platform was lengthened. To make the utmost use of the 280-ft long platform, the locomotive stopped just before the crossover, uncoupled, reversed over to the other road, moved forward and then a wire hawser with a hook at each end was linked between the drawbar of the locomotive and the coach axle. The driver then drew forward

Various railwaymen at Hotwells terminus in the 1890s.   *Author's Collection*

Access to Hotwells terminus, flooded 1909.   *Author's Collection*

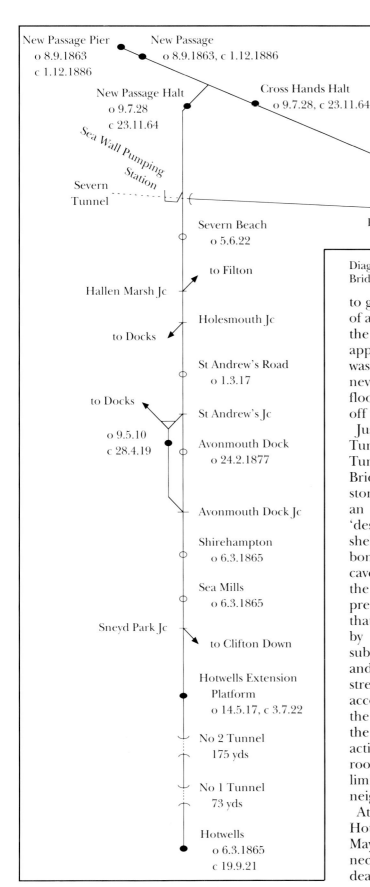

New Passage Pier
o 8.9.1863
c 1.12.1886

New Passage
o 8.9.1863, c 1.12.1886

Cross Hands Halt
o 9.7.28, c 23.11.64

Pilning Low Level
o 8.9.1863
c 1.12.1886
reopened 9.7.28
c 23.11.64

New Passage Halt
o 9.7.28
c 23.11.64

Sea Wall Pumping Station

Severn
Tunnel

Pilning High Level
o 1.12.1886

to Filton

Severn Beach
o 5.6.22

to Filton

Hallen Marsh Jc

Holesmouth Jc

to Docks

St Andrew's Road
o 1.3.17

to Docks

St Andrew's Jc

o 9.5.10
c 28.4.19

Avonmouth Dock
o 24.2.1877

Avonmouth Dock Jc

Shirehampton
o 6.3.1865

Sea Mills
o 6.3.1865

Sneyd Park Jc

to Clifton Down

Hotwells Extension
Platform
o 14.5.17, c 3.7.22

No 2 Tunnel
175 yds

No 1 Tunnel
73 yds

Hotwells
o 6.3.1865
c 19.9.21

Diagrammatic map of the route between Hotwells, Severn Bridge & Pilning

to gather up the slack and gently pulled the train of about six four-wheeled coaches into the station, the guard applying the brake when his van approached the platform. The locomotive shed was destroyed by fire on 27th March 1873 and was never rebuilt. On 12th January 1899, a high tide flooded the station, passengers having to be taken off the trains by boat.

Just beyond the station was the 73-yd long No 1 Tunnel, followed after a 30-yd break by No 2 Tunnel, 175 yds in length and situated below Bridge Valley Road. No 1 Tunnel was used for storing archives during WW2 while No 2 became an air raid shelter. Lord Horder said that it 'deserved full marks for having everything that a shelter should not possess'. If a high-explosive bomb had fallen above it, the roof would have caved in. The more its defects were emphasised, the more faith people had in it. Doctors were even pressed by their patients to give certificates stating that they had to be admitted. As well as being used by local residents, shelterers came from other suburbs such as Knowle, Southville, Bedminster and Stoke Bishop. Part of the tunnel was strengthened and illuminated and could accommodate about 200, but so many came that the unlit, unsafe portion beyond had to be used by the 2,500 to 3,000 occupants. Finally, official action was taken. The toilets were improved, the roof and walls strengthened and entry tickets limited to 400 given to residents of the neighbourhood.

At the far end of No 2 Tunnel, the 700-ft long Hotwells Extension Platform was opened on 14th May 1917 to handle war workers because the necessary train of eight coaches was too long to be dealt with at the terminus.

Ex-GWR single unit diesel railcars Nos W23W and W24W, with intermediate trailer, call at Sea Mills with an Up train in June 1957. The LMS maintained the signalling which explains the upper quadrant. *M G D Farr*

Sand drag near Sea Mills, 11th May 1954. Left-hand rails to Avonmouth, shining right-hand rails from Avonmouth. Should vehicles break away from the train they would be diverted by a spring point – out of the picture – on to the rusty rails which end at a sand trough, bringing them to a halt. *Dr A J G Dickens*

A short rise of 1 in 100 eased to 1 in 198 at the half-mile post, this gradient continuing to the three-quarter mile post where it fell at the same slope to Sneyd Park Junction. Following closure of the Hotwells line, the junction was taken out on 27th July 1924.

Sea Mills originally had one platform with a timber-built office and, like all original BPRP stations except that at Hotwells, faced south. When the line was doubled, the station was rebuilt in a domestic style of architecture. As Hotwells was an 'open' station, all tickets were collected at Sea Mills, though with the opening of Hotwells Extension Platform, they were inspected there. Sea Mills had no goods yard. A Sea Mills porter was responsible for washing rubbish out of the public subway following a high tide. The railway provided a hose pipe and wellington boots for him and the task was made more enjoyable by the fact that 'dirty money' was paid, the Shirehampton stationmaster in charge of Sea Mills checking each claim by reference to the tide book.

Beyond the station a 3-span 90-yd long viaduct crossed the River Trym and replaced an earlier structure of wrought iron and timber spans. On

Bristol (T.M.), Clifton Down and Avonmouth Dock, to Pilning Jct., Filton Jct., and Stoke Gifford.

Distance from				STATIONS.	Ruling Grad'nt 1 in.	Time Allowances for Freight Trains— (See also page 2).						J Goods.		J West Depot Goods.		J Weymouth Goods.		J West Depot Goods.		H Severn Tunnel Jct. Goods.	
Temple Meads (Mile Post).		Paddington via Box.				Point to Point Allowances.															
						Allow for Stop.	Allow for Start.	Vacuum.	D	Express.	Ordinary.										
M	C	M	C			Mins.	Mins.	Mins.	Mins.	Mins	Mins.	arr. a.m.	dep. a.m.	arr. a.m.	dep. a.m.	arr. a.m.	dep. a.m.	arr. a.m.	dep. a.m.	arr. a.m.	dep. a.m.
		118	28	**BRISTOL (T.M.)**																	
				Bristol (East Depot)		—	1														
				North Somerset Junction		1	1	2	2	2	3										
	43			Dr. Day's Bridge Sidings																	
	51	117	72	Dr. Day's Bridge Junction		1	1	2	2	2	2										
1	4	118	20	Lawrence Hill	200R	1	1	1	1	1	1										
1	50	118	67	STAPLETON ROAD	132R	1	1	2	2	2	3										
2	35	119	52	Ashley Hill Junction	75R																
2	65	120	2	Montpelier	77R	1	2	3	4	4	5										
3	23	120	40	Redland	77R			—	—	—	—										
3	71	121	8	**CLIFTON DOWN**	75R	1	2	3	4	4	5										
6	0	123	17	Sea Mills	I			—	—	—	—										
7	49	124	66	Shirehampton	100R	1	1	8	9	11	15										
8	31	125	48	Avonmouth Dock Junction	100F	1	1	2	2	2	3										
8	73	126	10	**AVONMOUTH OLD YARD**	L.	1	1	3	3	3	3	—	12 45	—	1 15	—	1 50	—	4 40	—	5 0
9	6	126	43	Gloucester Road Jct.	L.	1		1	1	1	1										
9	3	126	20	AVONMOUTH DOCK (Pass)	L.																
10	29	128	46	St. Andrew's Junction	L			—	—	—	—										
9	48			Avonmouth Tn. Gds. Yd.	L	1	1	3	4	4	5										
9	62			Avonmouth Gds. Yd. Jct.	L.			—	—	—	—	12 50		1 20		1 55		4 45			
				ROYAL EDWARD YARD	500R	1	1	4‡	4‡	4‡	5‡	12 52	1 15	1 22	1 50	1 57	2 37	4 47	5 15	5 7	5 30
9	76			St. Andrew's Road	L.			—	—	—	—			1 17		1 52		5 19			
10	51			Holesmouth Junction	500R			—	—	—	—					2 39					
				Avonmouth Factory Sdgs.				—	—	—	—										
10	74			Hallen Marsh Junction	100R	1	1	3	3	3	3		1 1?		1 53		2 40		5 20	C‡	34 S
13	45			**SEVERN BEACH**	200F	—	—	—	—	—	—	M X		M X		M X		M X		M X	
14	44			New Passage Halt		—	—	—	—	—	—										
14	79			Cross Hands Halt		—	—	—	—	—	—										
15	72			Pilning Low Level	L.	1	1	13	15	16	17									552 CR	L 6 25
16	27			Pilning Junction	100R	1	1	3	3	3	3									6 30	Z 6 50
14	5			Henbury	100R	1	1	6	7	8	10	—	—								
16	27			North Filton Platform				—	—	—	—										
16	38			Filton West Junction	100R	1	1	5	5	6	8		1 35		9 11		2 58		5 38		
17	15	—		Filton Junction Station	112R	1	1	2	3	3	4				2 15		3 2		5 42		
				STOKE GIFFORD	104R	1		4	4	4	6	1 40									

‡ From Avonmouth Old Yard

Working timetable for Bristol, Avonmouth and Severn Beach, 1938–9

The gas-lit Sea Mills booking office on 14th August 1960 with Edmondson ticket-dating machine, centre. Ticket racks on either side of the ticket window were concealed by a vertically sliding board.   *M G D Farr*

Shirehampton staff in CER uniform, c1900, with a mixture of MR and GWR bill boards. *Author's Collection*

the far side, the branch climbs at 1 in 100 round Horseshoe Bend before descending at 1 in 100 to Shirehampton station situated on the level. The original building was lengthened when the Down platform was added. As the station was the BPRP headquarters, its style of architecture was superior to that of the other stations. From 1875 the single road locomotive depot was at the east end of the layout until it closed in January 1905 when replaced by a shed at Avonmouth. During WW1, a remount depot was sited near the station and up to 60 wagons a day were dealt with – mostly wagons of hay or sawdust for the horses. About 12 wagons of manure were despatched daily, some going to Cadbury Road station on the Weston, Clevedon & Portishead Light Railway. When Nott Brodie won the contract for building Portway, he formed an end-on connection between the northernmost siding and his temporary light railway built for construction purposes.

The line falls beyond the station to Farr's level crossing, just before which a trailing siding ran to Crown Brickyard. Traffic from this siding to Bristol was required to be worked first to Avonmouth Dock Junction and then onwards by an Up train.

The original single platform Avonmouth Dock station, insufficient to deal with increasing traffic, was replaced by a larger one with two through platforms and a terminal bay opening on 1st September 1885. Between 1905 and 1924 it had a single road engine shed. Avonmouth was the BPRP's terminus and although originally provided with two platforms, the southern one fell out of use at an early date. Next to the station was a landing stage consisting of three pontoons reached from the shore by a 300-ft long pier supported on piles. The land being required for port development, the station was closed in 1903 and the terminus cut back to Avonmouth Dock. Quite a number of industries at Avonmouth were rail-connected, ICI and the Commonwealth Smelting Limited still using rail transport. From 1900 until 26th August 1964, boat trains were run in connection with ships to and from the West Indies. Banana traffic was heavy and in the week before the arrival of two banana boats, 700 vans needed to be strawed, weighed empty, steam heated to a temperature of 68 degrees Fahrenheit and weighed full. Wagons of loose straw, known to railwaymen as 'wagons of wind', came principally from stations on the Filton to Badminton line.

Shirehampton staff in front of signalbox, 1921. Note CER in block capitals on caps of the uniformed staff.   *Author's Collection*

Avonmouth Joint station, c1910.   *Author's Collection*

SS Ariguani discharging bananas at Avonmouth, 24th June 1947.

Port of Bristol Authority

PBA locomotive *Francis* at Avonmouth. The engine, built by Avonside, Bristol in 1901, was scrapped in 1952. *Author's Collection*

Banana specials were given running priority over most other trains. During both World Wars, Avonmouth was busy with troops, ammunition, aircraft, stores, locomotives, imported and exported. In the event of an air raid during WW2, a master switch could be thrown putting all the lights out. During one raid, a goods guard went to the locomotive footplate, the fireman closed the firebox door and they built a wall of coal on the front of the tender to provide shelter from blast or machine gun bullets. Until the 1930s, Avonmouth was used by emigrants, many foreign, 26,376 travelling by rail to Avonmouth in 1912. The GWR ruled that coaches used for this purpose should be disinfected as soon as possible after arrival and that after the emigrants left, each compartment be locked and not opened until so treated. Today there is no connection with the docks, whereas at one time the Port of Bristol Authority owned a large fleet of locomotives.

The Clifton Extension Railway had its own uniform consisting of a serge knee-length coat, long-sleeved waistcoat, trousers and cap. CER was embroidered on cap and coat in script, though later, metal cap badges were introduced with Roman letters, the lettering on the buttons remaining in script. The station-masters had gold braid on their uniform. During the post-grouping period, 'GW & LMS Jt' was embroidered on Great Western style hats.

Some of the employees were characters. Around the turn of the century a stationmaster at Sea Mills kept poultry, a cow and pigs, using his pony and trap to fetch swill from the docks. He sold eggs to passengers and provided the Superintendent at Bristol with butter and new-laid eggs. Another character was a driver nicknamed 'Mad Jack'. He enjoyed scaring dockers by rushing through the tunnels into Hotwells, but once misjudged his braking and crashed into the buffers.

Description of the line from Severn Beach to Pilning

Beyond Severn Beach, the single line continued and crossed the Severn Tunnel close to its eastern portal. It was just as well that the tunnel mouth was surrounded by a bank, as on several occasions, but for its protection, the sea would have entered the tunnel approach cuttings. Above the tunnel, until 1963, was a siding used by wagons taking coal to the Sea Wall Pumping Station, but the siding became redundant when electric pumps were installed. Beside the pumping station is the only true shingle beach in Gloucestershire – the material came from the Severn Tunnel excavations.

New Passage Halt opened in 1928 and about midway between New Passage and Cross Hands Halt, (the two were only about half a mile apart and both opened on the same day), was the site of the former Bristol & South Wales Union Railway to New Passage Pier. The track to Pilning Low Level followed the formation of the former BSWUR. When the Severn Tunnel was being built, one local recalled: 'The navvies would get in the Cross Hands at Redwick and have a booze-up. When they got merry they would vie with each other who would pay for the most quarts and tip them up, and the beer would be over the soles of their boots sometimes. At those times they didn't bother to unlace their boots, simply ran a knife down the laces and put in a fresh pair the next day'.

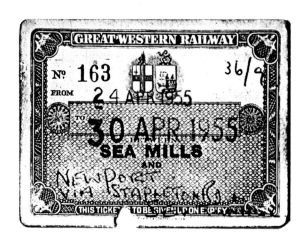

6. Bristol to Portishead

Like the Avonmouth line, the branch to Portishead was built to combat the problem of ships having difficulties navigating the Avon. In May 1845, Brunel conceived the idea of building a floating pier at Portbury and connecting it to Bristol by an atmospherically-worked railway similar to the one he was building in South Devon. It is interesting to note that an inclined plane worked by a winding engine was intended to connect the projected atmospheric railway with the then unfinished Clifton Suspension Bridge, thus tapping traffic from the other side of the river.

Although its Act of Parliament was granted in 1846, the Portbury Pier & Railway Company became a victim of the depression following the Railway Mania and was wound up in 1851. Twelve years later, the Bristol & Portishead Pier & Railway Company obtained Parliamentary powers to build a line from a junction with the Bristol & Exeter at Bedminster to a pier at Portbury, with a branch to the village, as it then was, of Portishead. This scheme was a rival undertaking to the Bristol Port Railway & Pier authorised the previous year, to run on the opposite bank of the river from Hotwells to Avonmouth. A change in plan caused the Portishead company to abandon the Portbury terminus and pier east of Portishead Pill. Instead, the proposed branch to Portishead became the main line and was extended to curve northwards across Portishead Pill to terminate at a new pier site on the pill – the local term for a creek or inlet.

The broad gauge single line was opened on 18th April 1867 with intermediate stations at Clifton Bridge, Pill and Portbury. Six trains ran each way on weekdays and one on Sundays, with a journey time from Bristol of 40 minutes. Passenger trains carried goods traffic until about July 1875.

The tidal portion of Portishead Pier was opened in June 1868 and the low water extension of 300 ft on 18th April 1870. Steamer services were operated by the railway to Cardiff and Newport (the Severn Tunnel had yet to be opened), and in the summer to Ilfracombe with through rail and steamer booking from the Great Western and Midland railways. The report for the half year ending 31st December 1881 stated that 165,882 passengers had been carried and the pier used by 32 steamers averaging 900 registered tons each, while 14 sailing vessels had berthed. The total for the whole year was 60 steamers and 16 sailing ships. In 1871 an Act was passed allowing Portishead Pill to be made into a dock. The BPRP on the opposite bank also had plans that year, so both were competing for a subscription of £100,000 from Bristol Corporation. The dock at Avonmouth was ready first and opened on 24th February 1877, but because of mishaps the Portishead Dock was not opened until 30th April 1879, the first ship to enter being the railway's steamer *Lyn* on 28th June 1879.

On 23rd June 1874 the branch had been used for an interesting experiment. An apparatus was tested for communicating between the guard and the driver, and between the passengers and the guard. This mechanism, designed by Reuben Lyon of Bristol, was fixed to three coaches. It consisted of a bellows and handle fixed to each compartment. By pulling down the handle, air was blown from the bellows through a pipe to the guard's box and blew whistles inserted into the ends of the pipes. In addition, the handle raised a signal arm, or a light at night, to indicate the compartment in which the apparatus had been used. This arm was so placed that it could not be

Portishead Pier and Railway, 1870.

Author's Collection

PORTISHEAD BRANCH. Narrow Gauge.

The Line from Bristol to Clifton Bridge is double, and from Clifton Bridge to Portishead single.

The Train Staff Stations are Clifton Bridge, Pill and Portishead. Pill is the intermediate crossing place.

Section.	Shape of Staff and Ticket.	Colour of Staff and Ticket.
Clifton Bridge and Pill	Triangular.	White.
Pill and Portishead	Round.	Blue.

Down Trains. BRISTOL TO PORTISHEAD.

Miles from Bristol.	STATIONS.	Week Days.																		Sundays.	
		1	2	3	4	5	6	7	8	9	10	11	12	13	14	15	16	17	18	1	2
		Goods	Pass.	Cond'l Goods	Pass.	Cond'l Goods	Pass.	Goods	Pass.	Cond'l Goods	Pass.	Pass.	Cond'l Goods	Pass.	Cond'l Goods	Pass.	Pass.			Pass.	
		A.M.	A.M.	A.M.	A.M.	A.M.	A.M.	A.M.	P.M.	P.M.	P.M.	P.M.	P.M.	P.M.	P.M.	P.M.	P.M.			P.M.	
—	**Bristol** .. dep.	..	6 55	..	7 45	..	10 10	..	12 45	..	2 45	3 50	..	5 25	..	7 20	8 30	..	..	3 45	..
¼	Pylle Hill ,,	5 45	—	7 0	—	9 20	—	10 50	—	1 30	—	—	4 50	—	6 10	—	—	....	....	—	....
1	Bedminster ,,	—	—	—	7 50	—	10 15	—	—	—	—	3 55	—	—	—	7 25	8 35	..	..	—	..
1¼	Malago Siding ,,	—	—	RR	—	RR	—	—	—	RR	—	—	RR	—	RR	—	—	....	....	—	....
2	Portishead Jun. ,,	5 50	7 0	7 5	7 55	9 25	10 30	10 55	12 50	1 35	2 50	4 0	4 55	5 30	6 15	7 30	8 40	..	..	3 50	..
3	Ashton Siding ,,	CR	—	—	—	—	—	CR	—	—	—	—	—	—	—	—	—	....	....	—	....
3½	Clifton Bridge ,,	6 5	7 5	7X30	8 0	CS	10 25	11X29	12X55	2X 0	2 55	4 5	5X 5	5 35	CS	7 35	8 45	..	..	3 57	..
7¾	Pill .... ,,	6 20	7X17	CS	8X12	CS	10X37	11 50	1 7	2X15	3 7	4X17	5 20	5 47	7X 0	7X47	8X57	....	....	4 11	....
9¾	Portbury .. ,,	6 35	7 25	—	8 20	—	10 45	CR	1 15	—	3 15	4 25	—	5 55	—	7 55	9 5	..	..	4 20	..
11¾	**Portishead** arr.	6 45	7 30	7 55	8 25	10 5	10 50	12 5	1 20	2 30	3 20	4 30	5 30	6 0	7 15	8 0	9 10	....	....	4 25	....

Up Trains. PORTISHEAD TO BRISTOL.

Miles from Portishead	STATIONS.	Week Days.																		Sundays.	
		1	2	3	4	5	6	7	8	9	10	11	12	13	14	15	16	17	18	1	2
		Pass.	Pass.	Pass.	Cond'l Goods	Pass.	Cond'l Goods	Pass.	Goods	Pass.	Cond'l Goods	Pass.	Pass.	Cond'l Goods	Pass.	Goods	Cond'l Goods			Pass.	
		A.M.	A.M.	A.M.	A.M.	A.M.	P.M.	P.M.	P.M.	P.M.	P.M.	P.M.	P.M.	P.M.	P.M.	P.M.	P.M.			P.M.	
	Portishead dep.	7 5	8 0	8 55	10 20	11 5	12 15	1 40	1 45	3 30	4 0	4 40	6 45	7 30	8 45	9 40	9 55	....	....	8 15	....
2	Portbury ,,	7 10	8 5	9 0	—	11 10	—	—	2 0	3 35	—	4 45	6 50	—	8 50	—	—	..	..	8 20	..
4	Pill .. ,,	7X17	8X16	9 7	10X58	11 17	CS	1 48	2X15	3 42	4X18	4 52	6X57	7X48	8X58	10 0	CS	....	....	8 25	....
8¼	Clifton Bridge ,,	7X29	8 28	9 17	CS	11X27	12X50	1X59	2 30	3 54	CS	5X4	7 8	8 10	9 10	10 20	CS	..	..	8 38	..
8¾	Ashton Siding ,,	—	—	—	—	—	—	—	CR	—	—	—	—	—	—	—	—	....	....	—	....
9¾	Portishead Jun. ,,	7 32	8 31	9 21	11 10	11 32	1 5	2 4	2 45	3 58	4 50	5 10	7 11	8 20	9 14	10 35	10 50	..	..	8 43	..
10½	Malago Siding ,,	—	—	—	RR	—	RR	—	CR	—	RR	—	—	RR	—	—	RR	....	....	—	....
10¾	Bedminster ,,	7 37	8 36	9 25	—	11 37	—	2 10	—	4 2	—	5 15	7 16	—	9 20	—	—	..	..	8 47	..
11	Pylle Hill arr.	—	—	—	11 15	—	1 10	—	3 10	—	4 55	—	—	8 25	—	10 40	10 55	....	....	—	....
11¾	**Bristol** arr.	7 40	8 40	9 30	..	11 40	—	2 15	..	4 5	..	5 19	7 20	..	9 25	..	..	..	..	8 50	..

CROSSING ARRANGEMENTS.

The 6.55 a.m. ex Bristol crosses the 7.5 a.m. ex Portishead at Pill.
The 7.0 a.m. RR ex Bristol will cross 7.5 a.m. ex Portishead at Clifton Bridge.
The 7.45 a.m. ,, ,, 8.0 a.m. ,, ,, Pill.
The 10.10 a.m. ex Bristol will cross the 10.20 a.m. RR ex Portishead at Pill.
The 10.50 a.m. ,, ,, 11.5 a.m. ex Portishead at Clifton Bridge.
The 12.45 p.m. ex Bristol crosses the 12.15 p.m. RR ex Portishead at Clifton Bridge.
The 1.30 p.m. RR ex Bristol crosses the 1.40 p.m. from Portishead at Clifton Bridge and 1.45 p.m. Train ex Portishead at Pill, when it runs.
The 3.50 p.m. ex Bristol crosses the 4.0 p.m. RR ex Portishead at Pill, when that Train runs.
The 4.50 p.m. RR ex Bristol crosses the 4.40 p.m. ex Portishead at Clifton Bridge, when it runs.
The 6.10 p.m. RR ex Bristol crosses the 6.45 p.m. ex Portishead at Pill.
The 7.20 p.m. ex Bristol crosses the 7.30 p.m. RR ex Portishead at Pill, when it runs.
The 8.30 p.m. ex Bristol crosses the 8.45 p.m. ex Portishead at Pill.

NOTE.—The loads of the Goods Trains not to exceed 26 Waggons.

The Portishead Goods Trains run through to the Great Western Yard.

Timetable for the Portishead branch, October 1886

lowered while the train was moving. The pipes doubled as a speaking tube between the guards, or between a guard and the driver. The inventor tried it with 300 ft of tube, equivalent to 10 or 12 coaches, and the six whistles invariably worked. Although seemingly successful, the invention was not generally adopted.

To cope with the increased traffic brought by the opening of the dock, the line from Bedminster Junction to Clifton Bridge was doubled, this being carried out with standard gauge, the branch having been narrowed between Saturday 24th January and Tuesday 27th January 1880. The doubling was completed on 2nd September 1883.

The GWR then agreed to purchase the railway and dock, this being authorised by an Act of 1884. The GWR abandoned the steamer services from Portishead on 1st October 1886.

On 8th July 1929 a half-hourly service was inaugurated, one train running from Temple Meads station and the other from Ashton Gate. Most of the trains crossed either at Pill or Portbury Shipyard signalbox. Because of this frequent service, a crossing loop was built at Oak Wood and the station at Portishead enlarged. In the 1950s, the power station at Portishead built by Bristol Corporation between 1926 and 1929 was extended by the British Electricity Authority which took over the site of the railway station and yard. A new station costing £250,000 was built nearer the town and opened on 4th January 1954. As a result of Dr Beeching's axe, passenger services were withdrawn on 7th September 1964, but freight traffic still continues to and from the docks, the Port of Bristol Authority having its own stud of locomotives there. Gradually freight decreased, cement being the only traffic in the final months, with the last train running to Portishead on 30th March 1981. Since then, occasional special Freightliner trains have been worked, containers being road-hauled from Portbury and placed on rail at Portishead. The line is at present retained out of use by BR as container traffic may increase and the line also figures in the Avon Metro scheme.

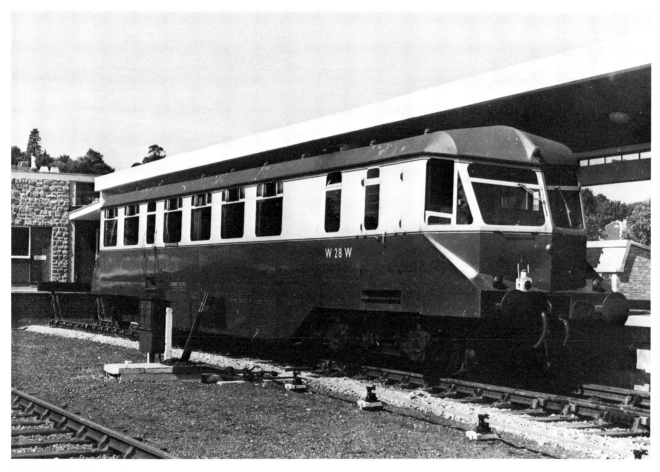

Ex-GWR diesel No W28W at the new Portishead station with the 1.45pm to Temple Meads. The ground frame for operating points can be seen in the foreground. 27th August 1954. *Hugh Ballantyne*

Description of the line from Bristol to Portishead

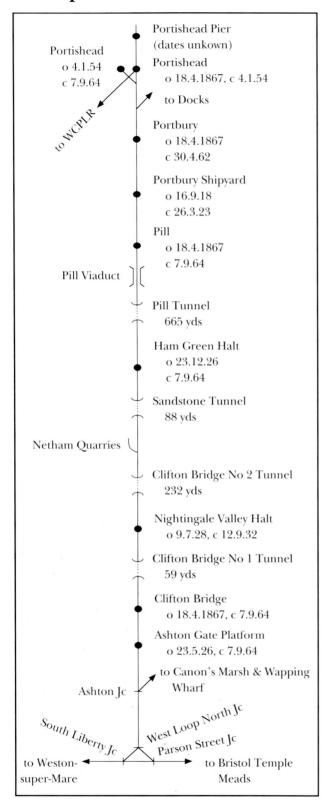

Diagrammatic map of the route from Parson Street Junction to Portishead

The Portishead branch leaves the Weston-super-Mare line at Parson Street Junction, (called Portishead Junction until 1932), curving northward to join the goods spur coming in from West Depot. Just before Ashton Gate, a branch curved off to serve Ashton Colliery. To the right are the Civil Engineer's sidings at Ashton Meadows where bridge and tunnel-gauging vehicles are stored. Ashton Gate Platform, close to Bristol City Football Ground, was opened on 15th September 1906 to cater for football crowds, and served by regular trains from 23rd May 1926. Sometimes football supporters' trains were hauled through from the SR by Bulleid Light pacifics. Following the general withdrawal of passenger trains on the branch, it enjoyed intermittent use by football specials between 1970 and 1977 and

ASSOCIATION FOOTBALL

1963/64 SEASON

Excursion bookings will be given in connection with Bristol City and Bristol Rovers away fixtures, forward and return by any train the same day. Special facilities will be advertised for F.A. Cup matches.

BRISTOL CITY

DATE	FIXTURE	STATION TO	FARE s. d.
Sat. 14 Sept.	Crewe Alex.	Crewe	32/6
„ 28 Sep.	Walsall	Walsall	25/0
„ 19 Oct.	Bournemouth	Bournemouth W.	16/9
„ 2 Nov.	Barnsley	Barnsley	42/0
„ 30 Nov.	Southend Utd.	Southend	35/0
„ 28 Dec.	Queens Park R.	Paddington	30/0
„ 4 Jan.	Colchester	Colchester	39/0
„ 11 Jan.	Notts County	Nottingham	33/6
„ 1 Feb.	Crystal Palace.	Paddington	30/0
„ 15 Feb.	Reading	Reading	20/0
„ 22 Feb.	Peterborough Utd.	Peterborough	45/0
„ 7 Mar.	Hull City	Hull	58/6(a)
„ 21 Mar.	Oldham	Oldham	41/0
Mon. 30 Mar.	Mansfield	Mansfield	37/6
Sat. 18 Apr.	Wrexham	Wrexham	35/0

a—Via Sheffield.

BRISTOL ROVERS

DATE	FIXTURE	STATION TO	FARE
Sat. 7 Sep.	Peterborough Utd.	Peterborough	45/0
„ 5 Oct.	Millwall	Paddington	30/0
„ 12 Oct.	Brentford	Paddington	30/0
„ 26 Oct.	Crystal Palace	Paddington	30/0
„ 9 Nov.	Reading	Reading	20/0
„ 23 Nov.	Coventry	Coventry	25/0
„ 21 Dec.	Oldham	Oldham	41/0
„ 18 Jan.	Southend Utd.	Southend	35/0
„ 25 Jan.	Notts County	Nottingham	33/6
„ 8 Feb.	Colchester	Colchester	39/0
„ 29 Feb.	Shrewsbury	Shrewsbury	27/6
„ 14 Mar	Walsall	Walsall	25/0
„ 28 Mar	Luton	Luton	34/0
„ 11 Apr.	Mansfield	Mansfield	37/6
„ 25 Apr.	Crewe Alex.	Crewe	32/6

TICKETS MAY BE OBTAINED IN ADVANCE FROM STATIONS AND AGENCIES.

FOR ENQUIRIES AT BRISTOL TEMPLE MEADS PLEASE RING BRISTOL 29-3451
Further information will be supplied on application to Stations Agencies or to Mr. D. S. HART, Divisional Manager Transom House, Victoria Street, Bristol 1 (Telephone 2-1001. Extension 664).

Bristol City/Bristol Rovers 1963–4 season excursions

Steam railmotor and trailer leave Ashton Gate with a Portishead to Bath train. Despite the word 'Halte' in the caption, as the GWR originally spelt it, the station nameboard in the picture reads 'Ashton Gate Platform'. This view was probably taken shortly after the platform opened in 1906. The line to the right curves round to Canon's Marsh and Wapping Wharf branches.

M J Tozer Collection

'Dean Goods' No 2426 at Ashton Gate carriage sidings in the early fifties.　　　　　　　*M E J Deane*

Clifton Bridge station, west. The arc-roofed canopies were rare in the Bristol area.

was re-opened temporarily for Dr Billy Graham's 'Mission England' held at the stadium from 12th to 19th May 1984.

Extensive sidings were situated on the right before Clifton Bridge station with its umbrella roofs sheltering the platforms. Its name changed to Rownham in 1891, but reverted to Clifton Bridge in 1910. The site is now the Headquarters of the Avon & Somerset Mounted Police. The signalbox was unusual in that it contained no less than three token instruments, (connected with Oakwood, Pill and Portishead boxes), so that one or both intermediate boxes could be switched out. Oakwood box only worked the morning shift, Pill closed overnight, while only Clifton Bridge and Portishead were manned for the full 24 hours.

From Clifton Bridge, the railway follows the foot of the Avon Gorge amidst picturesque scenery. Clifton Bridge No 1 Tunnel (59 yds long) passes under the abutment of Brunel's suspension bridge. Clauses in the original Act protected the interests of the bridge company, the railway running through a lined tunnel to satisfy its engineer. Beyond the tunnel, at the foot of Leigh Woods, was the delightfully named Nightingale Valley Halt, opened in 1928 and used for only five summers until its closure in 1932. Clifton Bridge No 2 Tunnel (232 yds) is unlined. Beyond was Netham Quarry box to give access to the quarry sidings and give warning of blasting. It was long disused before closure on 9th January 1922. Beyond the 88-yd long Sandstone Tunnel was Oakwood Crossing Loop. The amenities of Ham Green Estate were to have been preserved by the railway being placed in two tunnels, but while building the line, the tunnel proposed east of Ham Green Halt was replaced by a cutting. This unstaffed halt opened in 1926 to serve a large hospital. Beyond Pill Tunnel, 665 yds long, is the six-arch, brick-built Pill Viaduct.

West of Pill the line traverses flat country. Rather over a mile beyond the station was Portbury

Pill: 0-6-0PT No 7729 with the 1.00pm Saturdays-only Bristol to Portishead crosses dmu 55032 + 56292 working the 1.15pm Portishead to Bristol, 17th February 1962. *Hugh Ballantyne*

The domestic style of architecture is evident at Portbury station, 5th September 1958, looking towards Bristol. It is unusual in not having any posters, advertisements or timetables displayed. *Author*

Shipyard Loop. This was the remnant of a project begun in 1917 when a national shipyard was built at Portbury, but owing to the Armistice, it was left unfinished. The crossing loop and signalbox opened on 29th January 1918 and closed, but then re-opened again in 1928. Portbury Shipyard Platform, opened in 1918, remained in use until 1923. Latterly the site of the siding opposite the single platform at Portbury was converted into an attractive garden. The station closed in 1962.

The old station at Portishead was originally a single platform on the Down side and in 1929 a wood and cinder platform was built on the Up side. The Weston, Clevedon & Portishead Light Railway opened to the town on 1st September 1907 and a GWR siding made an end-on junction. The WCPLR closed on 18th May 1940. Beyond the GWR station was the Pier station, a line continuing along the pier itself, probably used by wagons coaling steamers. The main GWR

Portishead station was replaced in 1954 by one on a new site. The new Portishead station, designed by H E Cavenagh, was the Western Region's first in the post-war era. It was built of pre-stressed concrete and local limestone to blend with its surroundings. With the opening of this new station, passenger traffic increased as it was in a more central position than the old. Built on a marsh, problems of subsidence were experienced until its closure in 1964. Following the withdrawal of passenger traffic, the sidings were closed while the station building is now part of the Station Garage. There was a rail link to Portishead Docks worked by a stud of Port of Bristol Authority locomotives, but traffic is no longer railborne. In the 1960s, Albright & Wilson, manufacturers of phosphorus, distributed their product from Portishead in specially built rail tank wagons holding a payload of 22¼ tons each. As phosphorus was susceptible to spontaneous

PRIVATE AND NOT FOR PUBLICATION.   Notice No. 901.

GREAT WESTERN RAILWAY.

OPENING OF NEW STATION on the Portishead Branch on the Pill Side of Portbury Shipyard Exchange Sidings (mileage 127 m. 12½ chs.), to be named PORTBURY SHIPYARD PLATFORM, MONDAY, SEPTEMBER 16th, 1918.

This New Station, having access from the public road at Sheep House Lane Overbridge between Pill and Portbury, will be opened on Monday, September 16th, 1918, and passenger trains will be timed to call there in accordance with Public Bill No. B.890, and the working Time Table shewn below.

The platform is situated on the Up side of the Portishead Branch single line.

Passenger and parcels traffic of all descriptions will be dealt with.

The Station will be under the supervision of the Station Master at Portbury, and the trains and traffic will be attended to by the checkers working in turn at Portbury Shipyard Exchange Sidings, assisted, as may be necessary, by other members of the Portbury Staff.

Booking Clerks are requested to take care that correct tickets are issued to persons travelling to Portbury Shipyard Platform and Portbury respectively.

REVISED TIME TABLE OF PORTISHEAD BRANCH PASSENGER TRAINS.

DOWN TRAINS—WEEK DAYS.

Distance from Paddgtn. M	C		Pass.	Pass.	Mtr.	Pass.	Pass. SO	Mtr. VV	Pass.	Pass.	E'ty C'chs SX	Mtr.	Frome Pass.	Pass.	Pass. SO
			A.M.	A.M.	A.M.	P.M.	P.M.	P.M.	P.M.	P.M.	P.M.	P.M.	P.M.	P.M.	P.M.
118	28	Bristol (T. Mds.) dep.	7 0	8 20	9 50	12 15	..	2 5	4 15	5 30	..	6 30	7 50	9 25	11 0
119	32	Bedminster ,,	7 4	8 24	9 54	12 19	..	2 9	4 19	5 34	..	6 35	7 54	9 29	—
120	27	Portishead Jct. dep.	7 7	8 27	9 57	12 22	..	2 12	4 22	5 37	..	6 38	7 57	9 32	11 5
121	62	Clifton Bridge arr.	7 10	8 30	10 0	12 25	..	2 16	4 25	5 40	..	6 40	8 0	9 35	11 8
		Clifton Bridge dep.	7 14	8 32	10 2	12 27	..	2 17	4 26	5x43	6†15	6x43	8 1	9x36	11 10
126	13	Pill .. .. arr.	7x23	8x45	10 11	12 36	..	2 26	4 35	5x52	6†25	6 52	8 10	9 45	—
		Pill dep.	7 25	8x45	10 13	12 38	..	2 28	4x37	5 54	6x34	6 53	8 12	9 47	CS
127	12½	Portbury Shipyard Platform arr.	7 29	8 49	10 17	12 42	..	2 32	4 41	5 58	—	6 57	8 16	9 51	11 22
		Portbury Shipyard Platform dep.	7 31	8 50	10 18	12 43	1 24	2 33	4 42	5 59	—	6 58	8 17	9 52	11 26
127	46	Shipyard Sidings ,,	CS	CS	CS	CS	CS	CS	CS	CS	CS	CS	CS	CS	CS
127	77	Portbury arr.	7 33	8 52	10 20	12 45	1 26	2 35	4 44	6 1	—	7 0	8 19	9 54	—
		Portbury dep.	7 37	8 55	10 22	12 47	1 28	2 37	4 46	6 3	—	7 3	8 22	9 57	—
129	75	Portishead .. arr.	7 42	9 0	10 27	12 52	1 33	2 42	4 51	6 8	6†46	7 8	8 27	10 2	11 32

VV Will be train SO.

UP TRAINS—WEEK DAYS.

		Pass.	Pass.	Mtr. SO	Pass.	Pass.	Mtr. VV	Pass.	Pass. SX	Pass.	Mtr.	Pass.	E'ty C'chs SO	
		A.M.	A.M.	A.M.	P.M.	P.M.	P.M.	P.M.	P.M.	P.M.	P.M.	P.M.	P.M.	
Portishead .. .. .. dep.		7 10	8 30	10 45	12†55	1 10	3 5	5 15	5†35	6 18	7 20	9 10	11†45	..
Portbury .. .. ,,		7 15	8 35	10 50	—	1 15	3 10	5 20	—	6 23	7 25	9 15	—	..
Shipyard Sidings .. ,,		CS	CS	CS	1† 2	CS	CS	CS	CS	CS	CS	CS	CS	..
Portbury Shipyard Platform arr.		7 17	8 37	10 52	..	1 17	3 12	5 22	5†43	6 27	7 27	9 17	—	..
Portbury Shipyard Platform dep.		7 19	8 38	10 53	Q	1 19	3 13	5 23	5 48	6 29	7 28	9 18	—	..
Pill .. .. .. arr.		7x23	8 42	10 57	..	1 23	3 17	5 27	5x52	6x33	7 32	9 22	CS	..
Pill dep.		7 25	8x43	10 58	..	1 25	3 18	5 32	5 53	6 34	7 33	9 23	—	..
Clifton Bridge .. arr.		7 34	8 52	11 7	..	1 34	3 27	5x41	6 1	6x41	7 42	9x32	CS	..
Clifton Bridge dep.		7 35	8 54	11 8	..	1 35	3 29	5 43	—	6 44	7 44	9 34	CS	..
Portishead Jct. .. arr.		7 38	8 58	11 12	..	1 39	3 33	5 47	..	6 48	7 48	9 37	12 10	..
Bedminster.. .. arr.		7 41	9 1	11 15	..	1 42	3 36	5 50	..	6 50	7 51	9 41	—	..
Bedminster dep.		7 44	9 3	11 18	..	1 45	3 38	5 52	..	6 53	7 54	9 44	—	..
Bristol (T. Meads) .. arr.		7 48	9 7	11 22	..	1 49	3 42	5 57	..	6 57	7 58	9 48	12†14	..

Q To be run round in Exchange Sidings and backed to Shipyard Platform.   VV Will be train SO.

H. R. GRIFFITHS,

September 12th, 1918.   *Superintendent of Bristol Division.*

(700 R. 8vo.)   J. W. Arrowsmith Ltd., Quay Street, Bristol.

Announcement of the opening of Portbury Shipyard Platform with timetable of services

Portishead station, engine shed, goods yard and ship in dock on the left. There is a turntable beyond the shed in the centre foreground. View c1910.

Author's Collection

Exterior of Portishead station, c1905. *Author's Collection*

combustion in contact with air, it was loaded and discharged in water at a temperature of 60 degrees Centigrade. Full tank wagons travelled with a water 'blanket' and the tanks were filled with water for their return journey, both on safety grounds and to protect the tank shell from internal attack by acids formed from residues in the tanks. 36 to 40 tankers a week were handled.

In 1971 a woodpulp terminal opened at Portishead Dock and pulp was loaded direct into bulk trains to convey it to Marsh Ponds, east of Temple Meads, conveniently situated near the paper mill. This traffic had ceased by 1980 and branch closed on 3rd April 1981.

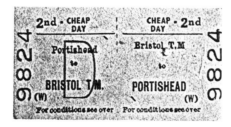

7. Bristol Harbour Lines

The first line to serve the docks at Bristol itself was the Bristol Harbour Railway built jointly by the Great Western, Bristol & Exeter and Bristol Corporation. It was an expensive three-quarters of a mile, requiring the demolition of a vicarage, the making of a cutting and a 282-yd long tunnel through a burial ground involving the expense of removal and re-interment at Arnos Vale on a plot of land purchased by the railway. The line also required the construction of a long viaduct and three bridges. The most interesting work was an opening bascule bridge over Bathurst Basin. Designed by Charles Richardson, mixed gauge was laid on its decking as both gauges were in use in the city. It was powered by a horizontal steam engine built by the Avonside Engine Company, Bristol in 1872 and now preserved in the Bristol Industrial Museum. The bridge was delicately balanced and in order that it could not be overdriven, was provided with a friction drive.

The Harbour line opened on 11th March 1872 and was extended to Wapping Wharf on 12th June 1876. On 4th October 1906 it was extended to Ashton Junction on the Portishead branch. Normally a goods-only line, when the main line to Weston-super-Mare was blocked between Temple Meads and Parson Street on Sundays 26th April and 15th November 1931 for two overline bridges to be demolished in order to further the work of quadrupling, passenger trains were diverted via this Harbour line. Following the demise of the city docks, the line fell out of use and was closed east of Wapping Wharf. Until fairly recently Wapping Wharf remained open for a daily coal train to Western Fuel Company's yard.

Although the Bristol Harbour line gave access to some shipping, it did not serve all the docks and in order to reduce barging and carting, in 1897 the GWR obtained powers to build an extension from Ashton Junction to Canon's Marsh where Bristol

Mrs Hare, Mayoress of Bristol, laying the first rail of the tramway on the Floating Harbour in connection with the Bristol & North Somerset Railway, 8th October 1863.

Courtesy *Illustrated London News*

Western Fuel Co's shunter at Wapping Wharf, 18th August 1980. It was originally the Port of Bristol Authority's No 30, built by Hudswell, Clarke & Co, 1959.
Author

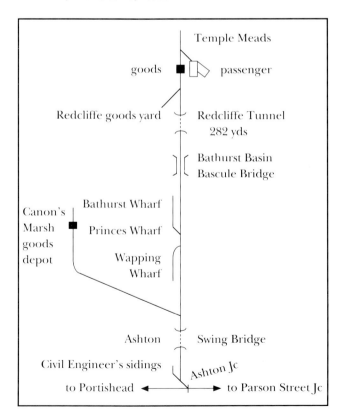

Diagrammatic map of the route from Ashton Junction to Canon's Marsh & Bristol Temple Meads

Corporation was spending £300,000 on deep water docks. As it was built on Cathedral land, the GWR was required to give an undertaking that no locomotive movements or whistling were carried out on Sundays during service hours. The line's most interesting feature was Ashton Swing Bridge. As a road bridge at this point was also needed, Bristol Corporation decided that the bridge would have two decks, the upper carrying the road and the lower a double track railway. Built by John Lysaght & Co Ltd for £70,389, its total length of 582 ft contained some 1500 tons of steelwork; the swing span alone, which was 202 ft long, weighing 1000 tons. The bridge was opened on 3rd October 1906. The swing span, which could turn either upstream or downstream, was moved by hydraulic power generated at the Underfall Yard. The two three-throw reversible engines working the bridge were situated in a control cabin above the roadway. Two vertical shafts turned the span, only one engine being required, the other acting as a stand-by. To prevent mishaps, the bridge was interlocked with the GWR signalboxes on either side making it impossible for signals to be lowered for the passage of a train unless the swing span was firmly secured.

As only one vessel was allowed to pass the bridge at a time, cones were provided to control shipping

BRISTOL HARBOUR RAILWAY.

The public are informed that the GREAT WESTERN and BRISTOL and EXETER RAILWAY COMPANIES are now prepared to convey TRAFFIC to or from the WHARF DEPOT near PRINCE's STREET BRIDGE (thereby affording convenient and speedy access to the FLOATING HARBOUR and DOCKS).

For particulars as to Rates, &c., apply to
Mr. HEARNE, Great Western Goods Station, Bristol;
or at either of the undermentioned Offices :—

ASSEMBLY ROOMS, Prince Street
UNIVERSAL OFFICE, High Street;
QUEEN's HEAD OFFICE, Redcliff Street.

N.B.—Until further notice no SINGLE Piece of TIMBER, MACHINERY, STONE, or any other Article exceeding TWO TONS in weight will be carried.

BY ORDER.

Notice re Bristol Harbour Railway from Bristol & Exeter timetable, 1877

Railway Correspondence & Travel Society's excursion crossing Ashton Swing Bridge, 26th September 1959. View north.
Dr A J G Dickens

RCTS excursion proceeding along Hotwell Road towards Canon's Marsh. Right is the training ship *Flying Fox*.   *Dr A J G Dickens*

movements. For vessels moving downstream, the north cone, point upwards, was lowered, with the south cone for those wishing to proceed up river. The yard arm on which the cones were hoisted was fixed so that both cones showed when the bridge was open. The bridgemaster had telephone communication with two stations, one upstream and one downstream about a quarter of a mile from his bridge, warning him at night, or in foggy weather, of the approach of vessels. The bridge, not swung since 1936, was made a permanent fixture in 1953. The control cabin and road deck were subsequently removed when a new road system to cope with modern traffic was constructed in the area.

The line which opened to Canon's Marsh in 1906 encouraged development. In addition to Bristol gas works which was given direct rail communication, it served a marble and slate importer, J S Fry & Son's chocolate factory and Messrs Rowe Brothers & Co Ltd's pipe and sheet lead works. Cattle could also be discharged here direct from ship to railway wagon and spared

being driven through the city for a mile or two. The 22 sidings in the yard accommodated a total of 531 wagons, about 550 wagons being exchanged daily. In 1914, 115 men were employed. The GWR goods shed and warehouse at Canon's Marsh, opened in October 1906, was of ferro-concrete. Measuring 540 ft by 133 ft, the 274 ferro-concrete piles averaged 32 ft in depth, due to the soft nature of the yard. It was built by Robertson of Bristol, the work being carried out under the supervision of P E Culverhouse. It could hold a total of 97 wagons. Loading and unloading was eased by the provision of eight electric cranes and three 30-cwt electric hoists. The upper floor of the shed was a warehouse.

Although most railwayman were honest, a few fell to temptation. During WW2 one shunter deliberately let a van containing sugar, then rationed, go hard up against a stop block knowing that something would break, thus allowing him to place a 'Not to Go' label on the van so that he could shunt it into the cripples' siding where he and his mates could help themselves to its contents.

(*Left*) Reproduction of the Bristol & Exeter Railway seal outside B&E House, Bristol.
Author
(*Below*) The Bristol & Exeter Railway offices, now B&E House, at Bristol, 23rd February 1990. Designed by F C Fripp, this Jacobean-style building was completed in October 1854.
Author

8. Bristol to Weston-super-Mare

In 1835 Parliament passed an Act authorising the construction of the GWR between Bristol and London and in October the same year, Bristol merchants formed another company to extend the line as far as Exeter. One of the advantages of this projected railway was that it would open up a 'vast coalfield' in the Nailsea–Backwell area. The Bristol & Exeter Railway, as it was known, obtained its Act the following year. Like the GWR, the B&E had Brunel as engineer and was built to the broad gauge. Four contracts were let in 1837, but then a financial depression caused difficulties in the payment of calls on the shares. The remainder of the contract for the line to Bridgwater was let in the spring of 1838. In 1839 the plan to have a temporary terminus at Pylle Hill was abandoned and it was decided to join the Great Western at Temple Meads. On 25th May 1841 thousands gathered to see *Fire Ball* (which by a coincidence had also hauled the first train between Bristol and Bath) leave with a trial train of eight coaches. Through being delayed 46 minutes at Bristol, the engine ran short of water and stopped at Nailsea to replenish its tender. A band playing 'See the conquering hero comes' greeted the train at Yatton and all along the line crowds waited to see it pass. Eventually it arrived at Bridgwater at 11.40 having taken 1 hour 54 minutes for the journey of 33¾ miles.

Many people had never seen a train before and did not know how to act. At the end of May, a country bumpkin saw a B&E train running on a trial trip. Saying, 'Dang un, I'll make un stop till I look at un', he threw a bar of wood across the track. The engine cut the bar in two and passed unharmed, but the company made an example of him by prosecuting. The B&E opened to the public on 14th June when the fares taken amounted to £302.

Weston-super-Mare was served by a 1½-mile long branch line and for ten years, three horses ridden by boys pulled the three railway coaches between Weston Junction and the terminus at Weston. Various accidents occurred both to the animals and their riders. From the beginning of 1848, as a result of a memorial presented to the railway, an Up morning train and a corresponding Down evening train were worked to and from Weston by a steam locomotive. For nearly three and a half years, steam and animal traction were in use together on the same line. In 1884 the branch was abandoned when the present Weston Loop line was opened to give through running to and from the West. Meanwhile in 1875, a third rail at standard gauge dimensions was laid between the broad gauge lines allowing trains of both gauges to use the track. In 1876 the GWR took over the B&E.

TRAIN SERVICE between CLIFTON DOWN and WESTON-SUPER-MARE.

DOWN. WEEK DAYS.	Mi. 1 2 a.m	1 2 3 a.m.	T 1 2 P a.m	1 2 3 a.m.	1 2 P a.m.	1 2 3 a.m	1 2 3 a.m	1 2 3 a.m	T 1 2 3 a.m	T 1 2 3 a.m	Fast 1 2 p.m	1 2 3 p.m
Clifton Down	..	6 55	..	..	..	8 35	9 30	..	10 25	11 25	..	..
Montpellier	..	6 58	..	..	..	8 38	9 33	..	10 28	11 28	..	..
Stapleton Road	..	7 3	..	..	..	8 43	9 38	..	10 33	11 33	..	..
Lawrence Hill	..	7 8	..	..	..	8 48	9 43	..	10 38	11 38	.	..
Bristol arr	..	7 15	..	..	..	8 55	9 50	..	10 45	11 45	..	..
Bristol dep	5 15	7 20	7 30	8 5	8 25	9 15	—	10 50	11 0	11 50	12 20	12 40
Bedminster	..	..	7 35	..	8 30	..	..	..	11 5	..	..	..
Bourton	..	..	7 49	..	8 42	..	..	..	11 16	..	..	..
Nailsea	..	..	7 55	..	8 52	..	..	..	11 25	..	..	..
Yatton	..	7 40	8 12	8 26	9 2	9 38	..	11 15	11 36	12 14	..	1 5
Clevedon dp	..	..	7 55	..	8 46	9 25	..	10 55	10 55	12 0	..	12 0
Clevedon ar	..	..	8 25	..	9 15	9 50	..	11 30	..	..	..	..
Worle	..	..	8 22	..	9 12	..	..	..	11 46	..	..	1 13
Weston Junction	5 43	7 57	8 31	..	9 22	9 49	..	11 30	11 56	12 30	12 48	1 19
Weston-s-Mare	5 58	8 6	9 10	..	9 28	10 0	..	11 40	12 2	12 35	1 0	1 34

DOWN. WEEK DAYS.	1 2 3 p.m	1 2 3 p.m.	1 2 3 p.m	1 2 3 p.m	T 1 2 3 p.m	1 2 3 p.m	1 2 3 p.m	Fast 1 2 p.m	T 1 2 3 p.m	1 2 3 p.m.	
Clifton Down	12 40	..	2 20	3 30	4 45	5 35	..	6 30	8 20	8 45	..
Montpellier	12 43	..	2 23	3 33	4 48	5 38	..	6 33	8 23	8 48	..
Stapleton Road	12 48	..	2 28	3 38	4 53	5 43	..	6 38	8 28	8 53	..
Lawrence Hill	12 53	..	2 33	3 43	4 58	5 48	..	6 43	8 33	8 58	..
Bristol arr	1 0	..	2 40	3 50	5 5	5 55	..	6 50	8 40	9 5	..
Bristol dep	1 40	3 0	3 15	4 40	5 15	6 0	..	8 15	8 50	—	..
Bedminster	1 45	..	1 2 Cls.	4 45	..	6 5	..	.	8 55	..	..
Bourton	1 54	..		4 56	..	6 19	..	..	9 3	..	..
Nailsea	2 3	..	3 35	5 4	..	6 27	..	..	9 10	..	..
Yatton	2 14	3 24	3 47	5 14	S	6 39	..	..	9 20	..	..
Clevedon dp	..	3 10	3 10	..	..	6 22	..	..	9 5	..	..
Clevedon ar	2 26	3 36	4 15	5 25	5 50	6 55	..	..	9 45	..	..
Worle	..	..	4 0	..	..	6 45	..	..	9 28	..	..
Weston Junction	..	3 45	4 11	..	5 44	7 0	..	..	9 38	..	..
Weston-s-Mare	..	3 50	4 21	..	5 50	7 10	..	8 50	9 45	..	..

DOWN. SUNDAYS.	1 2 P a.m	1 2 P p.m	1 2 3 p.m	1 2 3 p.m	1 2 3 p.m	1 3 3 p.m	FARES from CLIFTON DOWN. 1	2	3	Par	1 Ret.	2 Ret.
Clifton Down	..	2 30	4 0	5 30	6 30	8 15	..	..	..	..	..	..
Montpellier	..	2 33	4 3	5 33	6 33	8 18	0/3	0/2	0/1	0/1	0/5	0/[illegible]
Stapleton Road	..	2 38	4 8	5 38	6 38	8 23	0/6	0/4	0/3	0/2	0/9	0/6
Lawrence Hill	..	2 43	4 13	5 43	6 43	8 28	0/6	0/4	0/3	0/2½	0/9	0/6
Bristol arr	..	2 50	4 20	5 50	6 50	8 35	0/6	0/4	0/3	0/3	0/9	0/6
Bristol dep	6 30	3 30	—	—	—	—	..	..	..	..	..	..
Bedminster	..	..	1 2 3	..	..	..	..	..	..	..	..	..
Bourton	..	..		..	..	..	1/8	1/3	0/7½	0/7½	2/6	1/10
Nailsea	6 48	3 48		..	..	..	2/2	1/8	0/10	0/10	3/1	2/3
Yatton	6 59	3 59		..	..	..	3/0	2/4	1/2	1/2	4/3	3/1
Clevedon dp	6 47	3 45		..	..	..	3/0	2/4	1/6	1/6	4/3	3/1
Clevedon ar	7 10	4 15		..	..	..						
Worle	7 8	4 8		..	..	..	3/9	2/11	1/5½	1/5½	4/9	3/6
Weston Junction	7 17	4 17		..	..	..	..	..	..	..	..	..
Weston-s-Mare	7 27	4 30		..	..	..	4/3	3/4	1/10	1/10	5/9	4/2

UP. WEEK DAYS.	1 2 3 a.m.	M 1 2 P a.m.	1 2 3 a.m.	T 1 2 3 a.m.	1 2 P a.m.	M 1 2 P a.m.	T 1 2 3 a.m.	1 2 a.m.	1 2 P p.m.	1 2 p.m.	
Weston-s-Mare dep	..	6 40	..	8 40	..	8 20	10 0	10 40	..	12 11	..
Weston Junction	..	6 48	..	..	..	8 55	10 5	10 55	..	12 26	..
Worle	..	6 55	..	..	..	9 3	..	..	..	..	..
Yatton	..	7 6	..	..	9 0	9 13	10 17	11 10	12 12	..	..
Clevedon dep.	..	6 50	..	..	8 45	8 45	10 3	10 55	12 0	..	..
Clevedon arr.	..	7 18		..	..	9 50	10 30	11 30	.	..	..
Nailsea	..	7 14	..	..	9 10	9 21	..	11 23	12 22	..	..
Bourton	..	7 21	..	..	9 18	9 30	..	..	12 30	..	..
Bedminster	..	7 32	..	9 16	9 31	9 46	10 37	11 41	12 42	1 2	..
Bristol arr.	..	7 35	..	9 20	9 35	9 50	10 40	11 45	12 45	1 5	..
Bristol dep.	6 30	8 5	9 5	9 25	—	—	10 50	12 15	—	—	..
Lawrence Hill	..	8 10	9 10	..	.	..	10 55	12 20	1 2 3	..	..
Stapleton Road	..	8 15	9 15	..	..	..	11 0	12 25		..	..
Montpellier	6 40	8 20	9 20	9 35	..	..	11 5	12 30		..	..
Clifton Down arr.	6 45	8 25	9 25	9 40	..	..	11 10	12 35		..	..

UP. WEEK DAYS.	T 1 2 P p.m.	1 2 p.m.	1 2 P p.m.	T 1 2 P p.m.	1 2 3 p.m.	1 2 p.m.	1 2 P p.m.	T 1 2 3 p.m.	1 2 P p.m.	1 2 3 p.m.	
Weston-s-Mare dep	12 40	1 45	3 0	3 50	4 50	5 20	..	7 20	8 0	9 10	..
Weston Junction	12 47	1 58	3 14	3 55	4 56	5 32	..	7 26	8 12	9 19	..
Worle	12 56	1 2 3 from Bristol	3 25	4 5	..	..	..	7 32	8 21	..	..
Yatton	1 5		3 36	4 15	5 11	5 47	6 45	7 40	8 31	9 31	..
Clevedon dep.	..		3 10	..	4 55	5 27	6 25	..	8 15	9 5	..
Clevedon arr.	2 26		4 15	..	5 25	6 20	6 55	..	8 45	9 45	..
Nailsea	1 15		3 45	4 25	5 20	..	6 54	..	8 41	..	..
Bourton	1 23		3 55	4 33	5 28	..	7 1	..	8 50	..	..
Bedminster	1 37	2 32	4 11	4 47	5 42	6 11	7 16	8 2	9 5	9 52	..
Bristol arr.	1 40	2 35	4 16	4 50	5 45	6 15	7 20	8 5	9 10	9 55	..
Bristol dep.	1 50	3 0	4 10	5 5	6 5	1 2 3 Cls.	7 30	8 15	—	—	..
Lawrence Hill	1 55	3 5	4 15	5 10	6 10		7 35	8 20		..	..
Stapleton Road	2 0	3 10	4 20	5 15	6 15		7 40	8 25		..	..
Montpellier	2 5	3 15	4 25	5 20	6 20		7 45	8 30		..	..
Clifton Down arr.	2 10	3 20	4 30	5 25	6 25		7 50	8 35		..	..

UP. SUNDAYS.	1 2 P p.m.	1 2 3 p.m.	1 2 3 p.m.	1 2 3 p.m.	1 2 p.m.	From Weston-s-Mare. 1	2	3	Par	1 Ret.	2 Ret.
Weston-s-Mare dep	12 29	..	..	..	5 25						
Weston Junction	12 39	..	..	..	5 37	0/4	0/3	0/1½	..	0/6	0/4
Worle	12 48	..	..	..	..	1/0	0/9	0/4½	..	1/6	1/2
Yatton	12 56	..	..	..	5 49	1/8	1/4	0/8	..	2/4	1/9
Clevedon dep.	12 44	..	..	..	5 35	2/6	2/0	1/0	..	3/6	2/7
Clevedon arr.	1 8	..	..	..	6 1						
Nailsea	1 5	..	..	..	5 59	2/6	2/0	1/0	..	3/6	2/7
Bourton	..	..	..	..	..	3/0	2/6	1/2½	..	4/0	3/0
Bedminster	1 27	..	..	..	6 17	3/9	3 0	1/5	..	5/0	3/8
Bristol arr.	1 30	..	..	..	6 20	..	..	..	..	..	..
Bristol dep.	2 0	3 30	5 0	6 0	7 45	..	..	..	..	..	..
Lawrence Hill	2 5	3 35	5 5	6 5	7 50	..	..	..	..	..	..
Stapleton Road	2 10	3 40	5 10	6 10	7 55	..	..	..	..	..	..
Montpellier	2 15	3 45	5 15	6 15	8 0	4/3	3/4	1/10½	..	5/9	4/2
Clifton Down arr.	2 20	3 50	5 20	6 20	8 5	4/3	3/4	1/11	..	5/9	4/

S Slip Carriage detached at Yatton at 5 35 p.m. M Market Passengers conveyed to Bristol by these Trains on Thursdays. T These Trains run thro' without change of carriage at Bristol Joint Station or at Weston-super-Mare Junction. On Wednesdays a Train leaves Bristol for Yatton, Clevedon, Worle, Weston Junction and Weston-super-Mare at 11.30 p.m.

Timetable for Clifton Down to Weston-super-Mare, 1877

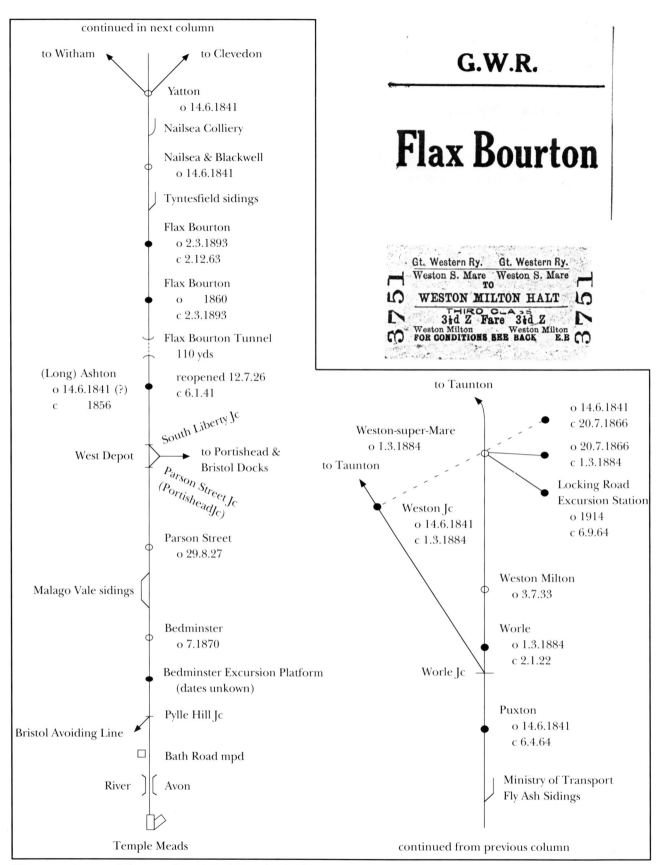

to Witham   to Clevedon

Yatton
o 14.6.1841

Nailsea Colliery

Nailsea & Blackwell
o 14.6.1841

Tyntesfield sidings

Flax Bourton
o 2.3.1893
c 2.12.63

Flax Bourton
o 1860
c 2.3.1893

Flax Bourton Tunnel
110 yds

(Long) Ashton   reopened 12.7.26
o 14.6.1841 (?)   c 6.1.41
c 1856

South Liberty Jc

West Depot   to Portishead &
              Bristol Docks
Parson Street Jc
(Portishead Jc)

Parson Street
o 29.8.27

Malago Vale sidings

Bedminster
o 7.1870

Bedminster Excursion Platform
(dates unkown)

Pylle Hill Jc

Bristol Avoiding Line

Bath Road mpd

River   Avon

Temple Meads

G.W.R.

Flax Bourton

Gt. Western Ry.   Gt. Western Ry.
Weston S. Mare   Weston S. Mare
TO
WESTON MILTON HALT
3751   THIRD CLASS   3751
3½d Z Fare 3½d Z
Weston Milton   Weston Milton
FOR CONDITIONS SEE BACK E.B

to Taunton

o 14.6.1841
c 20.7.1866

o 20.7.1866
c 1.3.1884

Weston-super-Mare
o 1.3.1884

Locking Road
Excursion Station
o 1914
c 6.9.64

to Taunton

Weston Jc
o 14.6.1841
c 1.3.1884

Weston Milton
o 3.7.33

Worle
o 1.3.1884
c 2.1.22

Worle Jc

Puxton
o 14.6.1841
c 6.4.64

Ministry of Transport
Fly Ash Sidings

continued from previous column

Diagrammatic map of the route from Bristol Temple Meads to Weston-super-Mare

Description of the line from Bristol to Weston-super-Mare

At first the B&E used the GWR's terminus at Bristol and this involved the cumbersome reversal either into or out of the station, but then in 1845 it opened its own terminus at right angles to the east end of the GWR station. The B&E train shed was a simple timber construction spanning two platform roads and two centre carriage sidings. Due to its unornate functional design and position near the Cattle Market, it was popularly known as the 'cow shed'. Although a double track curve linked with the GWR, an 'express platform' was only provided by the B&E on the Up line, but was used by through trains in both directions. The attractive stone B&E office block still stands to the south of the present station approach. It was designed by F C Fripp whose initials are high on the north side of the Jacobean style building completed in October 1854.

Contemporary painting by Harker of the Bristol & Exeter's train shed at Temple Meads. Notice that first class passengers use a different entrance from second and third class. *Author's Collection*

Leaving Temple Meads, Bath Road diesel depot is on the left. This is on the site of the former B&E locomotive works opened in January 1852. Overhauling engines initially, it built its first locomotive in 1859 and completed a further 34 during the next 16 years. As the company's main line was relatively short, 76 miles, the B&E tended to use tank engines, one express passenger class being most impressive with 8 ft 10 in-diameter flangeless driving wheels reaching almost to the top of the boiler. These driving wheels were the largest in regular use in Great Britain. B&E No 41, equipped with these large wheels, achieved a record speed of 81.8 mph down Wellington Bank in June 1854, this remaining for 36 years as the highest authenticated speed record.

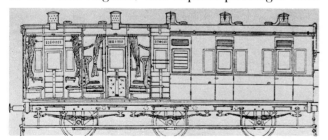

B&E composite coach built at Bristol in 1875. Second class compartment with less padding and leg room is on the left, with the more spacious and luxurious first class on each side of a centre luggage compartment. Courtesy *Railway Magazine*

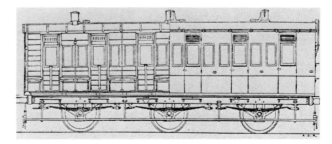

B&E third class coach built at Bristol in 1875. Passengers sit on wooden seats and have even less leg room than the second class. Courtesy *Railway Magazine*

B&E locomotive No 42 built at Bristol in 1868 with 8 ft 10 in diameter flangeless driving wheels. Converted to a tender locomotive in 1877, the year following the derailment at Flax Bourton of sister engine No 39 (re-numbered No 2001 by the GWR), she was finally withdrawn in 1889. It is not known what incident caused this damage to the bunker and buffer beam of No 42.

Author's Collection

No 3018 at Bristol shed on 18th May 1892. She was new and had only been completed at Swindon the previous month. Engines of this class were found to be too heavy at the front end, so the leading pair of wheels was replaced by a 4-wheel bogie. As well as being mechanically better, this gave the engine a more elegant appearance. Reconstructed in August 1894, she was named *Racer*. In both original and modified form, this type of engine almost monopolised the working of Paddington to Newton Abbot expresses via Bristol. By 1900, trains had grown too heavy for them and many of the class were withdrawn. No 3018 was renamed *Glenside* in 1911 and scrapped in 1913.

Rev A H Malan

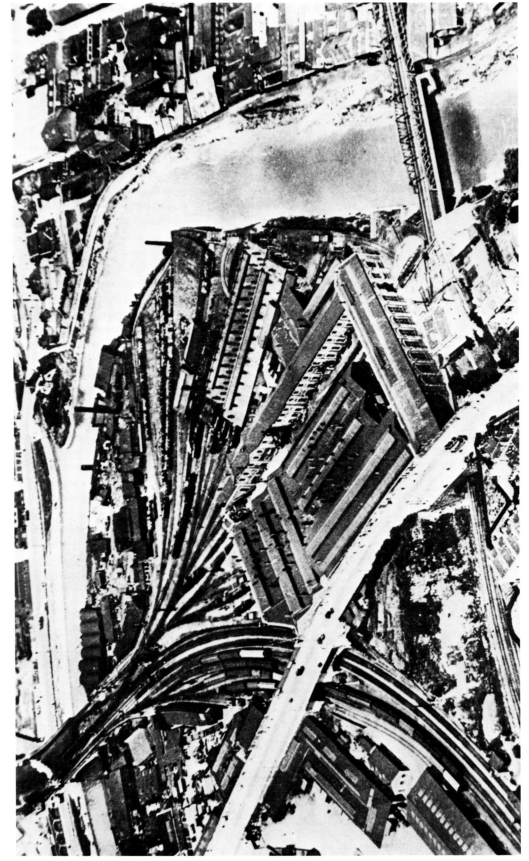

The GWR (former Bristol & Exeter) locomotive, carriage and wagon works, Bath Road, Bristol, c1930. Temple Meads passenger station is in the top left-hand corner, and the Bristol Avoiding Line in the foreground crosses the Avon, right.
M J Tozer Collection

LMS No 13197 works an Up LMS excursion from Weston-super-Mare through Long Ashton Halt in the early 1930s. *M E J Deane*

Beyond the Bath Road bridge is Pylle Hill, the former B&E goods depot, now used for parcels. Further west, just before Bedminster station was an excursion platform closed circa 1870. Bedminster station opened that year as a two-road station and had its platforms quadrupled in the 1930s. Continuing down the line, until recently Malago Vale carriage sidings were close to the site of the former Malago Vale Colliery. Parson Street station, opened in 1927 as Parson Street Platform, was replaced in 1933 by a four road station. During WW2 it is said that the driver of a Taunton to Bristol goods told the guard that he should ignore a stop at Parson Street station. When the train drew up there, the guard saw the driver climb in the 'station truck' immediately behind the engine and roll a cheese, then rationed, down the embankment to his home. An anthill diverted the cheese into a neighbour's greenhouse. To appease his neighbour's wrath, the driver agreed to share the cheese with him.

West of Parson Street is West Depot, part of which is now used as a Freightliner depot. At one time a branch led off at its far end to Ashton Vale Colliery. Ashton, closed by the B&E in 1856, was later the site of Long Ashton Platform opened in 1926. It had a comparatively short life and closed in 1941. Beyond the 110-yd long Flax Bourton Tunnel, unlined except at its ends which have a blue brick facing, was the first Flax Bourton station, closed in 1893 and replaced by another over a quarter of a mile further west. The waiting shelter of the 'new' station can now be seen on the Down platform at Crowcombe on the West Somerset Railway. Flax Bourton had a mail exchange apparatus. To the west are Tyntesfield sidings laid by the Ministry of Fuel & Power in 1956–1957 and now retained out of use.

Nailsea & Backwell, simply Nailsea until 1st May 1905, was fairly recently refurbished by BR and Avon County Council jointly. Like Flax Bourton it had mail exchange apparatus, as did Yatton, at one time an important junction with branches to Clevedon, the Cheddar Valley and Wrington, but Beeching cuts in the sixties reduced it to the status of an ordinary station. Here, Brunel differed from

131

Nailsea & Backwell station, c1920. Most of the platform is of timber – a relatively light construction was required, it being built on an embankment. Right is the stationmaster with row of fire buckets behind available in the event of the platform igniting. A milk churn stands at each end of the building and the two porters are also well spaced out. A permanent way man wearing a straw hat stands in the Up road, while the signalman has all the windows open, leans out, duster in hand, watching the photographer. The signalman arrived on a bicycle, parked near the steps to his box. Between the main station building and signalbox is the goods shed. In more recent years the platform was replaced in concrete.

Author's Collection

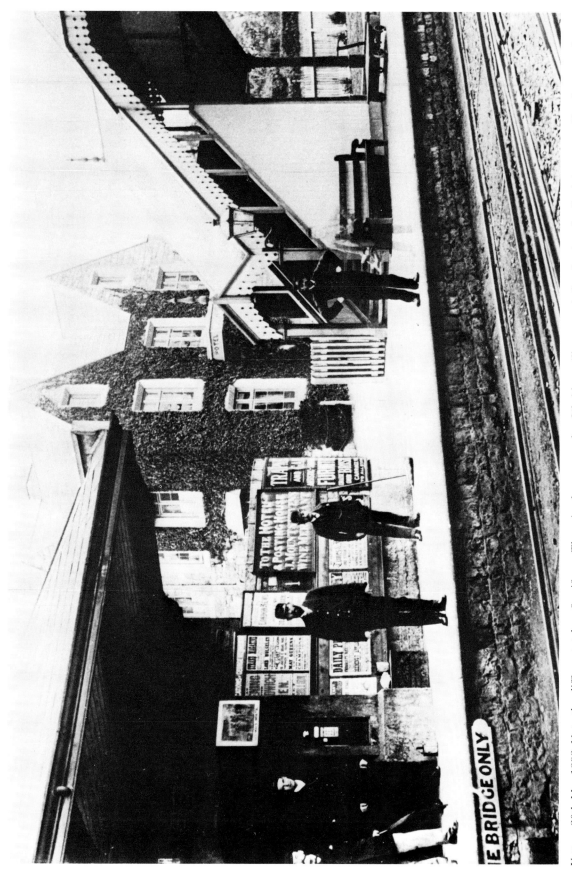

Yatton, 20th May 1892. Note the different styles of uniform. The mixed gauge track, of 'bridge rail' pattern, is fixed to longitudinal sleepers unlike the normal cross-sleepers of standard gauge track. The back of the seat near the foot of the bridge steps bears the words 'Yatton Station'. Railway servants cross over the track from one platform to another – note the step on the far left – but passengers are requested to use the bridge. There is a GPO box in the wall. It enjoys three collections daily, weekdays-only. On the original photograph, in the stonework above the door can be traced the letters 'Booking Office'. To the right of the door is a box for collecting used books and magazines. The name of the charity cannot be read. Advertisements include those for the *Strand Magazine, Illustrated London News, Bristol Times & Mirror* and the adjacent Hotel and Posting House.

Rev A H Malan

his usual practice in having a building on one platform different from that on the other. On the Down side is a Tudor building with a flat, all-round awning, while that on the Up has an Italianate hipped roof with Tudor details. About 1941, a bomb dropped between the Up and Down main lines between Yatton and Huish Crossing. Trains were diverted, at least one express travelling from Witham to Yatton. For about 24 hours, all four tracks were closed, but the next day the Up and Down loops could be used to pass traffic going slowly past the crater.

Puxton, as well has having goods sidings, also had a line serving the milk depot using rail-borne tankers. The station had quite a few changes in nomenclature. Opened as Banwell, it was renamed Worle in 1869, became Puxton in 1884 and finally Puxton & Worle in 1922. At the time of writing, Avon County Council and BR have proposed a new Worle station about a third of a mile east of Worle Junction. The old Worle station, immediately beyond the bifurcation of the Exeter and Weston-super-Mare lines, opened in 1884 on the new Weston-super-Mare loop line, and closed

GWR parcels way bill for an item from Bristol to Clevedon Road, as Yatton was called before the Clevedon Branch was opened. Parcel was to Mr Offer at Clevedon. It was received by the railway at noon on 4th May 1846. The charge was three shillings. *Author's Collection*

Nos D6984 and D6975 backing into West Huish fly ash sidings with a train from Aberthaw. The ash is for use in constructing the M5. 10th September 1970. *Hugh Ballantyne*

Up 'Cornishman' passing Worle signalbox, 3rd May 1892. Worle station on the Weston-super-Mare loop can be seen immediately to the left of the signalbox. The track is mixed gauge.   *Rev A H Malan*

in 1922, though the disused buildings and platforms lasted for over another 40 years. As an economy measure, Weston loop was singled in 1972. Weston Milton Halt, opened in 1933 to serve a growing suburb, was refurbished by BR and Avon County Council in 1983.

Weston-super-Mare was one of the first seaside resorts to be served by a railway. In 1844, 23,000 visitors arrived by rail, an increase of 300 per cent over the coaching era five years previously. Its station has had quite an involved history. The original terminus in Alexandra Parade was

The original Weston-super-Mare station in what is now Alexandra Parade. The train is horse-drawn. The drawing was made in 1846.   *Author's Collection*

A busy scene at Weston-super-Mare, c1905. A train of empty coaching stock stands on the middle road; on the right a passenger train is facing Bristol, while in the bay platform is another passenger train. It is probably headed by a 'Metro' tank engine with steam blowing from its safety valves. Notice the attractive shape of the roof canopy.

Lens of Sutton

replaced in 1866 by a larger station, this being relegated to goods use when the Weston loop replaced the former Weston branch, the loop line requiring a through, not terminal, station. Part of the former Weston branch remained as a siding to the gas works. The delightful through station in pale grey local stone was designed by the B&E's engineer Francis Fox. It has a pleasant exterior canopy, while the ridge and furrow roof above the sharply curved platforms is impressive. It is supported on decorated lattice girders and the tapered columns are embellished by a spiral design at the base and acanthus leaves on the capitals.

Additionally, in 1866, an excursion platform was built in Locking Road beside the then new terminus. Improved in 1914 and enlarged to four platforms in 1922, this station was used mainly in the summer, but finally closed in 1964. The excursion platform was certainly well used because on a Bank Holiday Monday the GWR and LMS (LMS engines worked through to Weston-super-Mare) would bring over 30,000 passengers in 30 special trains and the normal two-road station could not have coped with such traffic. In the first half of the 20th century, Weston was very popular for Sunday School excursions, about 4,000 children travelling there on 29th June 1909 and a total of 76,000 in June and July 1912. Although the excursion platforms were rather bare, it was not necessary to have protection against winter weather. The excursion platform was used, rather surprisingly, as the starting point and terminus of the prestigious 'Bristolian' on summer Saturdays in 1952.

9. Bristol to Pensford

Radstock was reached by rail from Frome in 1854 and plans were drawn up for extending the line to Bristol. The outcome was that the Bristol & North Somerset Railway was empowered by an Act of 1863 to construct a line connecting the MR and GWR at Bristol with Radstock where it was to climb over the Mendips to a junction near Bruton with the Somerset Central Railway, one of the constituent companies of the Somerset & Dorset Railway whose Bath Extension had yet to be built.

On 7th October 1863 the first turf of the BNSR was turned at Clutton, but soon, owing to financial difficulties, the contractor Bethel & Watson stopped work. A second, William Lawrence, came on the field and works were carried further, only to be suspended again. Circumstances were not assisted when in 1870 J Bingham, the company's secretary who had run up large bills for legal and Parliamentary expenses, was sentenced to 12 months' imprisonment with hard labour for attempting to defraud the company's Bristol banker, W M Baillie. A third contractor, Perry & Co of Bow completed the line, the work delayed when heavy rain during the winter of 1871–2 caused landslides. It opened from Bristol to Radstock on 3rd September 1873, the GWR absorbing the company on 1st July 1884.

The branch closed to passenger traffic on 2nd November 1959 and after a flood washed away part of the Radstock to Bristol line on 10th July 1968 this section was closed completely and Radstock coal travelled a circuitous route via Frome and Bath to Portishead power station and Imperial Smelting Processes Ltd of Avonmouth.

BRISTOL, RADSTOCK AND FROME.

STATIONS.		K Goods	B Pass.	K Goods	K Westbury Coal.	B Pass.	B Pass.	B Pass.	B Pass. SO	B Pass. U	B Pass. U	B Pass.	B Pass.
		p.m.	p.m.	p.m.	p.m.	p.m.	p.m.	p.m.	p.m.	a.m.	p.m.	p.m.	p.m.
BRISTOL (T.M.)	dep.		5 20			6 20	7 55	9 53	11 20	9 40	2 40	4 50	8 20
East Depot	"	3 35											
Marsh Junction	"	CS	CS			CS	CS	CS	—	CS	CS	CS	CS
Brislington	"	RR	5 27			6 27	8 2	10 0	—	9 47	2 47	4 57	8 27
Whitchurch Halt	"		5 34			6 34	8 9	10 7	11 34	9 54	2 54	5 4	8 34
Stop Board	"	4 P0	—			—							
Pensford	arr.	4 10	5X40			6X40	8X15	10 13	11 40	10 0	3 0	5 10	8 40
Pensford	dep.	4X15	5 41			6 41	8 16	10 14	11 41	10 1	3X 1	5 11	8 41
Pensford and Bromley Siding	arr.	SO	—			CS							
	dep.												
Clutton	arr.	4 31	5 49			6 49	8 24	10X22	11 49	10 9	3 9	5 19	8 49
Clutton	dep.	4X47	5 50			6 50	8 25	10 23	11 50	10 10	3 10	5 20	8 50
Stop Board	"	4 P56											
Hallatrow	arr.	5 2	5 53			6 53	8 28	10 25	11 53	10 13	3 13	5 23	8 53
Hallatrow	dep.	5X29	5 54			6X54	8 29	10 27	11 54	10 14	3 14	5 24	8 54
Stop Board	"	5 P38											
Farrington Gurney		—	5 58			6 58	8 33	10 31	11 59	10 18	3 18	5 28	8 58
Old Mills Siding	arr.	—	—			—							
	dep.	—											
Midsomer Norton and Welton	arr.	—	6 1			7 1	8 36	10 34	12 2	10 21	3 21	5 31	9 1
	dep.		6 2			7 2	8 37	10 35	12 3	10 22	3 22	5 32	9 2
RADSTOCK	arr.	5 52	6 5	RR		7 5	8 40	10 38	12 7	10 25	3 25	5 35	9 5
RADSTOCK	dep.		6 7	6 50		7 8	8 41	10 39	12 8	10 26	3 26	5 36	9 6
Mells Road	arr.		6 14	7 8		7 15	8X48	10 46	—	10 33	3 33	5 43	9 13
Mells Road	dep.		6X17		6 40	7 16	8 50	10 47	CS	10 34	3 34	5 44	9 14
Stop Board	"		—		6 P50	—							
Somerset Quarries Siding	"					—							
Gas Works Siding	"					—							
Market Siding	"					—							
Frome Mineral Junction	arr.		CS		7 6	CS	CS	CS	CS	CS	CS	CS	CS
FROME	arr.		6 27			7 26	9 0	10 57	12‡30	10 44	3 44	5 54	9 24
FROME	dep.		6 39										

Working timetable for Bristol to Frome, 1938–9

Description of the line from Bristol to Pensford

Passenger trains started from Temple Meads, followed the London line to North Somerset Junction, then curved south to Marsh Junction where the line from East Depot Junction came in. Almost immediately the line bifurcated, the Bristol Avoiding Line curving right and the Radstock line left past Marsh Pond carriage sidings. The Avoiding Line, opened on 10th April 1892, joins the Weston-super-Mare line at Pylle Hill Junction and allows non-stop trains to skirt Temple Meads. It was particularly useful before Temple Meads was extended in the thirties, and on busy summer Saturdays, trains full of holidaymakers to and from the south-west travelled by this route, often changing locomotives at St Philip's Marsh depot which catered for goods, as opposed to passenger engines which were shedded at Bath Road. Saturday specials were often worked by mixed traffic engines which during the week had been hauling freight trains. St Philip's Marsh engine shed, opened in 1910 and closed in 1964, was the second largest depot on the GWR. 28 roads radiated from each of the two turntables, while additionally there was a two-road repair shop with an extra section added where the GWR diesel railcars were maintained by AEC fitters. Owing to the fact that the depot was built on 'made' ground, the rail surface being some 30 ft above the natural ground level, piling was used to support the buildings. These piles were ferro-concrete and it was the first time that such piling on the Hennebique system had been used for a Great Western engine shed. Demolished in 1965, a wholesale fruit and vegetable market was built on the site.

Near Marsh Junction is a three-road HST maintenance depot opened in September 1975 and recently lengthened to cope with longer trains. It has a bright, cheerful appearance helped by the white floor which encourages staff to keep their footwear clean and not carry dirt into a train. The concept of the shed is that the whole train is serviced on one site, instead of locomotives and passenger coaches being serviced in different sheds. The former St Philip's Marsh goods yard, renamed Victoria sidings, is used for overnight stabling of HSTs.

Beyond Marsh Junction the Radstock line crossed the 73-yd long Avon Viaduct and climbed at 1 in 62 to Brislington, the only station, as distinct from a halt, on the branch, which was not a block post.

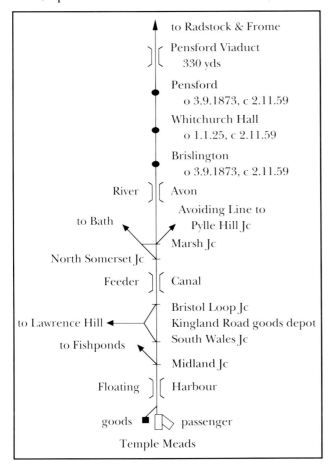

Diagrammatic map of the route from Bristol to Pensford

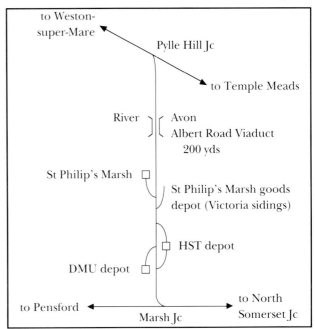

Diagrammatic map of the Bristol Temple Meads Avoiding Line

0-6-0PT No 9669 arriving at Brislington from Temple Meads on 28th March 1959 with a train to Frome. A coal wagon, left, was a feature of most station yards before the days when central heating became general. A folded tarpaulin is in the left foreground. This would have protected goods conveyed in an open wagon.
R E Toop

Brislington station, c1905, looking towards Bristol. This rural station is most attractive with a garden on the right, while ivy and rambler roses climb over the buildings.
M J Tozer Collection

Whitchurch Halt with its attractive pagoda: BR Standard Class 3MT 2-6-2T No 89040 passes with the 10.50am Frome to Bristol on 31st October 1959. *Hugh Ballantyne*

No 4593 at Pensford with the 10.50am Frome to Bristol stopping train on 10th October 1959. The signalman holds the single line tablet on his shoulder. The right-hand platform appears to have been raised at some period.

Hugh Ballantyne

Pensford Viaduct: No 4536 leaving Pensford with the 6.15pm Bristol Temple Meads to Frome on 1st September 1953.   *Author*

The opening of an electric tramway in 1900 creamed off quite a number of passengers from the railway. The line climbed at 1 in 60 through Whitchurch Halt, opened in 1925, to a summit near Maes Knoll. At the head of all steep gradients on the branch were boards requiring goods and mineral trains to stop and pin down their wagon brakes. The line fell at 1 in 66 to Pensford which, unlike Brislington and Whitchurch, had two passenger platforms and a goods shed, the latter destroyed by a stray bomb in WW2 and not rebuilt until 1958. Beyond the station was the impressive 330-yd Pensford Viaduct, a Grade II listed building. The most expensive feature of the line, it had 16 arches, and the rail level was 95 ft above the ground.

The branch was sometimes used by through trains – in 1933, for instance, by a summer Saturday train from Birmingham to Weymouth, while in the fifties a Frome to Bristol train carrying express headlights conveyed passengers off the Up Channel Islands express out of Weymouth and stopped only at Radstock and Pensford in order to allow passengers to catch the 7.15pm Bristol to Manchester and Glasgow and the 7.25pm to Newcastle-upon-Tyne.

In April 1958 the line between Marsh Junction and Pensford was used for testing two railbus chassis built at the Bristol Commercial Vehicle Ltd's works which backed on to the line at Brislington. Following these trials, the chassis were taken by road to Lowestoft where Eastern Carriage Works 56-seater bodies, very similar to their bus design, were added. The railbuses then worked in Scotland. These vehicles might have proved a great success, but did not. Although capable of carrying normal traffic, their failing was that a sudden increase in the number of passengers meant that a normal-sized dmu had to be used and it was uneconomic to keep a standard dmu just on stand-by. A further reason for their demise was that freight services were soon withdrawn from the branches the railbuses served and as the freight's share of track upkeep was therefore unavailable, income from railbuses was insufficient to bear the cost alone. Had they been developed 20 years earlier it could have been a different story.

Pensford Viaduct; No 3440 *City of Truro* heads southwards with the RCTS 'North Somerset' rail tour on 28th April 1957, assisted by 2-6-2T No 5528 which in true GWR fashion is placed 'inside' the train engine. No 5528 is ex-works and painted in the green lined livery permitted that year to many classes hitherto black, or lined black.   *Hugh Ballantyne*

Composite picture: Pensford Viaduct bathed in sunshine on a winter's morning, c1905

Pensford Viaduct: BR Standard Class 3MT 2-6-2T No 82033 crosses the viaduct with the 10.50am Frome to Bristol Temple Meads on 29th October 1959, during the last week of passenger service. Notice the low telegraph poles across the viaduct. *Author*

ar right is the passenger station, then the signalbox, goods shed and rake of wagons. *Author's Collection*

10. Accidents and Mishaps

The length between Bristol and Bath has had more than its share of accidents. The first of any significance occurred at Saltford on 18th July 1845. In the evening, the tyre came off a driving wheel of the locomotive hauling an Up timber train just before Saltford Tunnel and getting under the train de-railed the last wagon on to the Down line. The locomotive of the 2.00pm passenger train from Paddington mounted the de-railed timber wagon, the passenger coaches staying on the track due to the inherent stability of the broad gauge. The fireman was thrown off the footplate and dislocated his shoulder. A special train was sent from Bristol to collect the passengers. As only the Up line could be used until the disabled stock was removed, in order to prevent trains colliding head-on, a pilot engine was used between Saltford and Keynsham. The Down line was re-opened about 24 hours after the de-railment. The engine suffered only superficial damage, though, to quote the *Bath Chronicle*, 'some of its external works and ornamental appendages were much injured'.

March 1849 proved unlucky for trains in the Keynsham area. As the 7.30pm from Bristol to Bath was approaching Keynsham on the 14th, the engine became detached from the coaches. Unfortunately the driver was not aware of this. As he drew to a scheduled stop at the station, his train, still going at a considerable speed, surprised him by crashing into his engine. 20 passengers were cut and bruised.

When the Down express reached Fox's Wood on the evening of the 21st, it collided at 40 mph with some goods wagons left on the rails. The three-inch thick buffer beam on the engine was smashed as also were the goods trucks. The passengers were only shaken. It was another good advertisement for the broad gauge that the train was not de-railed.

Fox's Wood was the scene of another collision just over two years later. At 3.00am on Sunday 10th August 1851, a 6-coach excursion train carrying visitors returning from the Great Exhibition in London left Bath. Two minutes after its departure a tank engine arrived which had assisted a goods train through Box Tunnel. It was properly detained for 20 minutes and left at 3.23am. Meanwhile the engine of the excursion had made good progress as far as Twerton where it exhibited unmistakable signs of distress. It was coaxed

through Keynsham, but the driver thought that the feed pumps had failed and being afraid of an explosion, drew to a halt outside Bristol No 3 Tunnel. Just before it stopped, the tank engine struck its rear at approximately 15 mph. About 20 passengers were injured, but none seriously. The last coach escaped much damage because it was a strong second class vehicle with an iron frame. The crew of the tank engine were taken into custody and pleaded guilty – an inspector believed they were asleep. Charged before the magistrates at the Lamb Inn, Keynsham, the driver was fined £5 and the fireman £3. Their respective wages were 5s 6d and 3s a day.

In the early morning of 7th June 1865 a collision near Keynsham injured 14 passengers. A double-headed express stopped owing to fancied engine trouble and was about to proceed when the postal train ran into it. The disaster was compounded when, in the confusion, an empty carriage train ran into the back of the Mail. When the coaches of the express reached Bristol, a dead Shetland pony was found lying on the roof of a first class coach where it had been thrown by the force of the collision. Three men in the last compartment of the last coach had a fortunate escape as the doors were at that period locked, but one of them chanced to have a carriage key. When the first train stopped, the guard, following regulations, went back to protect it and when called by the engine whistle left a fusee, an appliance like a Roman candle which when struck smartly burned for ten minutes. It could be seen for a considerable distance and was a caution signal to indicate that a train had left within ten minutes. The guard of the mail was stunned by the first collision and had got back only about 150 yds to try and protect his train when the third train passed. Both trains had been kept at Bath for ten minutes and as there were no signals between Bath and Bristol at night, there was no means of preserving the time interval.

On the Up side of the track near the western mouth of Bristol No 2 Tunnel is a stone, set on a plinth. It has had the honour of being featured in Hansard. Just before 2.00pm on 31st March 1876, a passing local Up train dislodged a large boulder from the quarry's stack beside the line. A few minutes later the Down 'Flying Dutchman' approached at 50 mph. As it emerged from Bristol No 3 Tunnel, the fireman saw this stone lying across the Down track. He also saw a man trying to shift it. This he succeeded in doing, but in saving dozens of passengers from death or injury had the train been de-railed and plunged into the Avon, he lost his own life because before he could jump clear, the engine struck him a fatal blow.

This brave man was Jack Chiddy, foreman at the adjacent Birchwood Quarry. When the train stopped, a collection among passengers raised £3 17s 0d – little compensation for his wife and seven children who had now lost their breadwinner. The case was taken up in Parliament by Lord Elcho who said that if a man risked his life to save others, he should do so 'with the consciousness that his family would not be dependent on charity or the workhouse'. The Chancellor of the Exchequer explained that the Government had no funds available to help such people and that the GWR should be approached to make the family an allowance. The ensuing press publicity resulted in a fund being opened in Bath and another in Bristol, the Bank of England contributing £10 when informed that two of its officials were on the train with a large quantitiy of gold. £400 was raised and used to purchase half an acre of land on which Memorial Cottage was built in what is now Memorial Road on the opposite bank of the river. On the north side of the six-bedroomed house is a tablet bearing the inscription: 'Erected AD 1877 by public subscriptions for the widow and family of John Chiddy who was killed by an express train whilst removing a large stone from the metals of the Great Western Railway near Conham, March 31, 1876'.

On 27th February 1900 the 6.02pm Down fast from Bath ran into a landslide of 10,000 tons of earth and stone covering the Down line for 40 yds immediately east of the east portal of Saltford Tunnel. The locomotive was de-railed and with four of the coaches, thrown over to the Up line. Fortunately the train was running late and had therefore passed the Up train before it reached the landslip. The line being impassable until noon the following day, passengers walked by the landslip to join a train the other side of the tunnel. To clear the obstruction 100 men had ropes attached to their waists, with the other ends fastened to strong stakes driven into the field above. They worked night and day by the light of naphtha flares. On two occasions trucks being filled with fallen earth were buried by a further slide, and stout chains, used to try and pull them clear, snapped under the strain of the locomotives pulling them.

St Anne's Park was the scene of another mishap. At 2.15pm on 11th January 1967, the 11.45am Paddington to Bristol express was standing at a signal when it was struck in the rear, between No 3 and No 2 Tunnels, by the 12.45pm Paddington to Swansea which had been diverted via Bath to avoid a freight train derailment at Westerleigh East Junction. The collision caused 13 passengers to suffer minor injuries. The rear coach of the Bristol train was struck by 'Western' class diesel-hydraulic No D1071 *Western Renown*. 'Warship' class diesel-hydraulic No D864 *Zambesi*, running by light on the Up line, was also slightly damaged when it scraped against the Bristol train's last coach. Long distance trains were diverted via Badminton, local passengers being catered for by a shuttle bus service set up between Bath and Bristol, up to 12 vehicles being used. The line was cleared at 9.15pm.

There was the making of a serious accident at Mangotsfield on 30th August 1886. A weekly excursion train run from Gloucester to Weston-super-Mare was approaching Mangotsfield North Junction. A goods train down the line towards Bath mistook the signalman's indication for the passenger train to come on, for a sign for the goods to reverse. The engine of the excursion and two or three coaches passed safely, but then the brake van of the goods train just fouled the main line and carriage after carriage scraped the van, their panels being damaged and their steps smashed. No passenger was hurt apart from Kathleen Organ, a thirteen-year old girl who had her hand out of the window and received a cut. After it was dressed at the Bristol General Hospital she was able to continue with her journey, the Superintendent at Bristol kindly extending the validity of her return ticket for a few days in case she decided to rest at Weston-super-Mare for a while. Less fortunate was James Quick the passenger guard, whose protruding ducket was cut off causing him to be thrown violently to the floor. His mouth was badly injured and he received severe cuts to his head. Taken to Bristol General Hospital, he lay unconscious for about ten hours.

On 30th September 1949, Class 5 4-6-0 No 44745 was hauling the 1.58pm parcels train from Derby to Bristol and as it passed Westerleigh North sidings at high speed at about 7.30pm, it came in contact with the open door of a banana van which was stationary on the Up line. The fireman, who was sitting on a seat looking over the side of the cab, received a blow on the head and died two

Flax Bourton accident, 27th July 1876. A not-too-accurate drawing: the smoke box door is too small and the two cylinder covers are not precisely placed. The locomotive's number appears to be on the front of the tender, which being a tank engine, it did not have!

Courtesy *Illustrated London News*

hours later. Members of Westerleigh staff had been known to open doors of banana vans to search for fruit overlooked when unloading and the Ministry of Transport Report placed responsibility for the accident on the unknown person who had failed to fasten the doors on the last occasion they were opened; superelevation on the curve caused the insecure door to swing open.

A fire at Horfield Halt on Friday 13th April 1934 completely destroyed the ticket office apart from its steel safe. The halt closed at 10.30pm and the fire was spotted at 12.30am by a signalman in his box several hundred yards away. He alerted the fire brigade. It was believed that an oil stove had set the office alight.

On 27th July 1876 Driver William Dunscombe left Taunton 20 minutes late with the Up 'Flying Dutchman', the fastest train in the world. His engine was 4-2-4T No 2001 built at Bristol eight years previously. Although late, Dunscombe believed that all was not lost, because the line between Taunton and Bristol was an ideal galloping ground since it was level and mainly straight, enabling him to maintain a speed of about 60 mph. Having regained three of the lost minutes, while descending the incline of 1 in 180 on the Bristol side of Flax Bourton Tunnel the oscillation of the engine became violent and by Goston's Bridge the locomotive mounted the right-hand rail, ran along its top surface for about 12 yards and then jumped off the track. It ran along the six-foot gap between the Up and Down tracks for 30 yds, then cut through the Down line, carrying away transoms and sleepers. Even so, the engine still had sufficient impetus to carry on for another 50 yds where it plunged against a steep embankment, falling on to the line and turning over lengthwise.

Fortunately the chain coupling the train to the engine broke, the coaches passing the derailed engine, and the leading guard's van crashing into the embankment on the Down side of the line and throwing John Watts, the guard, onto the opposite embankment. Watts, despite a broken arm, sprained ankle and cuts, had the presence of mind to collect two red flags from his wrecked van and gave them to passengers so that they could walk along the line on either side of the smash to warn approaching trains, for debris blocked both lines. They succeeded in stopping the next Down train which pulled up in 200 yds and averted a further tragedy.

James Randall, fireman of No 2001, was killed instantly, being almost disembowelled and the back of his head cut off. Driver Dunscombe was fatally injured having lost an arm and leg, dying about 20 minutes after the crash. Both were Bristol men. The passengers were fortunate to get off lightly, though their luck was no doubt due in no small measure to the solidarity and stability of the broad gauge. Only the first coach was derailed, but a number of passengers cut themselves slightly when climbing out through the carriage windows after having smashed them first. This was in some cases their only exit, quite a few of the doors being locked on both sides of the carriage. Fourteen passengers complained of injury and were taken to Long Ashton where they were received most hospitably by the villagers. One injured passenger, initially offered a derisory shilling compensation by the GWR, had this raised to £450 by the Courts.

The cause of the accident? It was difficult to attribute any fault to the locomotive as it had only come out of Swindon workshops 12 days before, having undergone overhaul since 20th March. The jury at the inquest blamed the uneven permanent way, the gangers claiming that there had been a deficiency of materials for maintaining the line. The Great Western had taken over from the Bristol & Exeter six months previously. The latter company had not wanted to spend any more on the line than was thought necessary as it was to be handed over to another company, and the Great Western had failed to get supplies through to its new acquisition quickly enough. Although No 2001 was re-railed some 30 hours after the accident, she was so badly damaged that she had to be scrapped. The following year the three engines of the same class were converted to tender engines, as opinion changed and tank engines were not considered suitable for hauling express trains.

On 20th March 1855 an accident occurred not to a train, but to a barge taking coke, the smokeless fuel used by locomotives of the period, to the Bristol & Exeter Railway's wharf at Bristol. The large flat-bottomed barge *John*, propelled by auxiliary steam power and belonging to Messrs Insall & Co, patent coke manufacturers of Cardiff, had discharged 130 tons of coke and left to go down river at 10.00am. As it had been an unusually high tide, the ebb was strong, while the boat was unladen, light and therefore difficult to steer. Its Master, apprehensive that she would strike the piers of the B&E bridge south of Temple Meads station, had a warp thrown out to bring the bows round and reversed his engine. The vessel struck the bridge without causing damage and went on. The tide being high, it struck the cast iron girders of Bath Bridge, causing the whole structure to fall across her bows and then sink. The vessel carried on down to Bedminster Bridge, of the same design as Bath Bridge, and although struck, this held firm.

11. Bristol Locomotive Builders

It is not generally realised that locomotive building was an important Bristol industry and that between 1864 and 1881, no less than one in nine of the engines built in Britain were constructed at Bristol, while approximately 4,200 were built in the city between 1837 and 1958.

The first locomotive builder in Bristol was Henry Asprey Stothert, son of George Stothert, owner of a foundry at Bath. Henry established his business in 1837 at Avonside Wharf next to the Bristol & Gloucestershire Railway which brought him coal, the Floating Harbour giving him convenient access to water transport for incoming pig iron, and for the despatch of locomotives. His works built engines for the GWR, B&E and South Devon Railway, as well as other companies, and flourished by providing good work at low prices. Two years after founding his business, Henry took as partner, Edward Slaughter, assistant engineer to Brunel. To keep the works going when orders for locomotives were slack, they also manufactured

marine engines, steam pumps and point capstans. In 1856 Henry Grüning joined the firm; Stothert having retired, the firms's name changed to Slaughter, Grüning & Co. To raise additional capital the firm became a limited company in 1864, being re-styled the Avonside Engine Company. Its six directors included William Bevan, chairman; Henry Grüning; Alfred Sacré, younger brother of Charles Sacré, locomotive superintendent of the Manchester, Sheffield & Lincolnshire Railway; Edward Slaughter; and soap manufacturer Christopher Thomas. The first exported engine went to Tuscany in 1847. Slaughter, Grüning & Co built for the GWR, among other engines, 26 broad gauge locomotives of the 'Hawthorn' class, one being named *Slaughter*. However, an engine bearing this name did not instill confidence in passengers, so it was changed to *Avonside*. In 1871, Avonside built under licence articulated engines to the design of Robert Fairlie, engines of this pattern working on

Avonside erecting shop, 1905. Burry Port & Gwendraeth Valley Railway No 5 *Cwm Mawr* (it later became GWR No 2195 and worked on the Weymouth Quay Tramway). The two smaller engines beyond are Great Northern Railway railmotor engines Nos 7 & 8.

Author's Collection

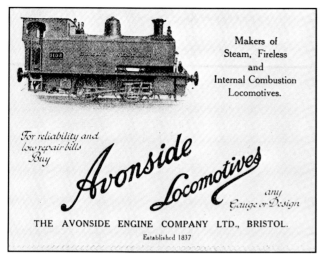

Avonside advertisement. *M J Tozer Collection*

Fox looked after the financial side and Walker the engineering affairs. Their works was established at Deep Pit Road, St George, access to the adjacent Midland main line being via the colliery branch. From 1864 to 1878 the factory was called the Atlas Engineering Works. The firm hoped to exploit a 'Steep Gradient Locomotive' patented by Henry Handyside in 1873 and tested in the construction of Avonmouth Docks. Locomotives of this type were able to climb a gradient of 1 in 10 by gripping a centre rail but this interesting idea was never marketed successfully. In December 1878 the firm of Fox, Walker & Co was wound up due to the depression in the industry.

Five months later Avonside too succumbed, was reconstituted but forced into liquidation in July 1881. That same year the Atlas Engineering Works was taken over by Thomas Peckett who continued building industrial locomotives.

In August 1882 Edwin Walker acquired Avonside's machinery, patterns and spares and leased part of the former works and continued to build locomotives. He was innovative – as early as 1902 the company built an internal combustion

the Festiniog Railway. By the mid-seventies the firm employed a workforce of 800–900 building about 50 locomotives a year.

In 1864 two Quakers, Francis William Fox (cousin to the Francis Fox, engineer to the B&E) and Edwin Walker, founded Fox, Walker & Co to specialise in the building of industrial locomotives.

Inside the Atlas Works: in the foreground are partly completed saddle tanks to fit over boilers in the background.
Author's Collection

DELIVERY AND SHIPMENT.

Every locomotive passes the most rigid inspection during building, and on completion is thoroughly tested under steam on a special railroad of various gauges and different gradients we have specially laid down for the purpose.

Locomotives for use in this country, after being tested, are sent out in charge of one of our experienced men, who, upon arrival at its destination, starts the locomotive and leaves everything in proper working order, to the satisfaction of the buyer or his representative. Locomotives for shipment, after completion and trial in steam, are carefully taken to pieces, all bright parts coated with Rust Preventive Composition, and packed by experienced packers in cases rendered watertight by strips fastened over the joints with marine glue, or in zinc-lined cases.

All cases are stoutly made and battened and hooped with iron. Boilers and frames are boarded or protected by battens where necessary. Driving wheels and other parts not requiring complete boxing are wrapped and protected from injury at the journals and crank pins. All boxes and packages are distinctly and permanently marked with the proper shipping marks, numbers, dimensions, and weights.

PRICES.

It will be noticed that we give in this List as much information as possible, with the exception of prices.

Prices are necessarily dependent upon the fluctuations of the market, and if printed in this List would very soon be out of date and misleading.

We shall be pleased to give quotations on application for locomotives suitable for any gauge of railway or class of work, constructed for burning Coal, Wood, or Oil as fuel, together with photographs and full specifications.

Our prices, we think, will compare very favourably with those of other Makers. It has always been our endeavour to maintain the highest standard of excellence, for which we have the reputation in the past, and to reduce the cost to the lowest point, by the best possible system, facilities, and management; and by using only the very best materials and workmanship obtainable, and the most efficient designs, to give thorough satisfaction to every customer.

We shall be pleased to give references to users of our locomotives all over the country. In this connection we are pleased to say that more than half of our orders are repeat orders from old customers; of many of the rest of our orders, they are largely influenced by personal knowledge of our work.

Two pages from a Peckett & Sons' locomotive catalogue. *Author's Collection*

STANDARDISATION OF PARTS.

We have already referred to the fact that all our productions are standardised. By means of Gauges and Templates, and special tools and machinery, each locomotive is made interchangeable with all others of the same size and class. This system of manufacture is a distinctive feature of these Works. Like parts will therefore fit accurately in all engines of the same class. The value and importance of this system to the users of locomotives cannot be over-estimated.

Every important part of the locomotive being accurately made to a template, we can at any time supply a duplicate part made to the same template, which is sure to fit in the place of the original, so that customers can have their engines duplicated in whole or in parts. The large number of locomotives at all times in progress of our principal classes, insures unusual and especial facilities for despatching at once orders for duplicate parts.

Duplicate parts, such as :—Boilers, Fire Boxes, Brass Tubes, Wheels and Axles, Tyres, Crank Pins, Axle Boxes and Brasses, Connecting and Coupling Rod Brasses, Side Rods fitted complete, Cylinders, Cylinder Covers, Piston Rods, Piston Rings, Injectors, Injector Steam and Feed Cocks, Water Gauges, Crossheads, Slide Bars, Steam Pipes, Exhaust Pipes, Whistles, etc., etc., we always keep in stock ready for immediate delivery.

In ordering duplicate parts all that we require is the number of the engine, which will be found stamped on all the working parts ; also whether right-hand or left-hand (this is determined by standing in the cab and looking towards the chimney) ; no sketches or dimensions are required.

When a single locomotive is depended upon, and where the stoppage of the locomotive may involve a shut down and the idleness of a large number of men, our having a large stock of duplicate parts at hand is of great importance to our customers ; we send any of the above parts off the same day as the order is received.

CALCULATING TRACTIVE FORCE.

Satisfactory results depend upon the tractive force and the weight on the coupled wheels of a locomotive being properly proportioned. Thus, if the weight be too small, the locomotive is over-cylindered and the wheels will slip too easily. If the weight be too great the engine is under-cylindered, which means so much dead weight to be moved about without any advantage to the engine. In adjusting the best proportion of tractive force and weight, due regard has to be paid to the character of work for which the engine is intended. Thus, for instance, passenger and goods traffic usually require a driving weight of about five times the tractive force. The tractive force given in the following pages is based on a working pressure of 160-lbs. per square inch with 70 per cent. cut-off.

REPAIRS.

We should strongly advise the owners of a locomotive, especially where shop facilities are not easily available, to employ as an Engineer a man who is sufficiently competent to keep up all small running adjustments and repairs.

In course of time, even with the best of usage, the boiler and machinery of any locomotive will require general repairs and renewals. Having extensive workshops and every convenience, we are prepared to do work of this kind promptly, and we use our best judgment to keep the cost as low as can be, consistent with a thorough and satisfactory job. We shall be pleased at any time to give an estimate for any repairs required.

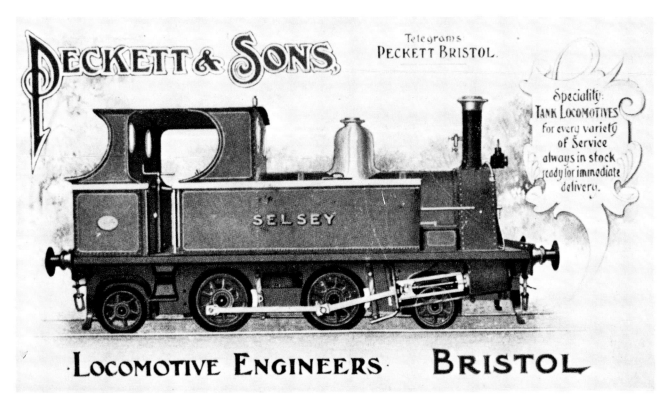

Two advertisements for Peckett & Sons' locomotives.

M J Tozer Collection

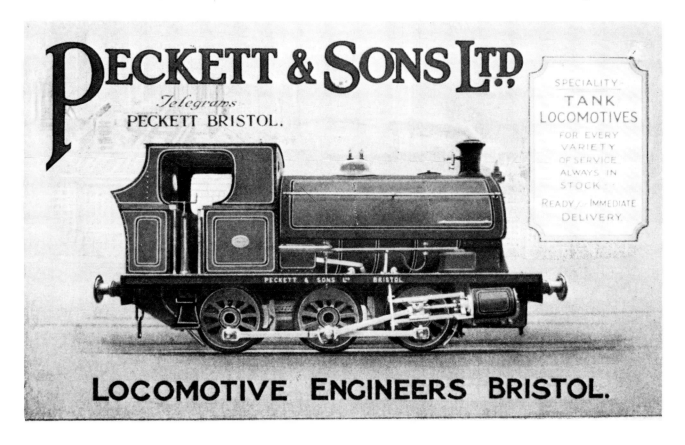

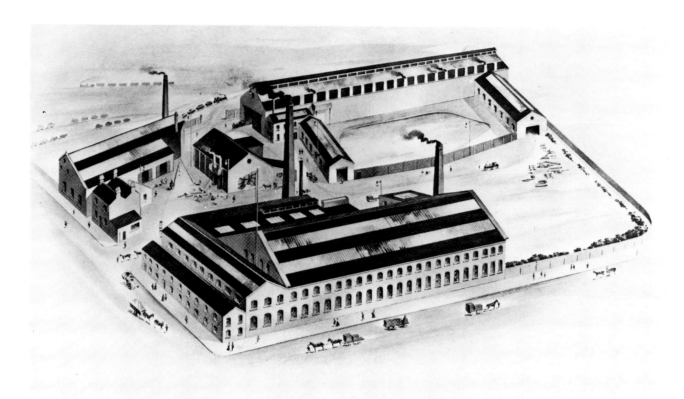

BIRD'S-EYE VIEW OF WORKS, COVERING 5 ACRES.
(Covered area, 101,800 square feet, with a further 8 acres for extension).

Peckett's Atlas Locomotive Works.

M J Tozer Collection

engine locomotive for use in the Transvaal. Business generally expanded and in 1904 Walker took Ronald Murray as a partner who was able to provide capital for a new factory at Fishponds where a maximum of 300 were employed. The Depression in the 1930s caused the company to fail, going into liquidation on 29th November 1934 and the works closing early in 1935. The company's goodwill, drawings, patterns and spares were acquired by the Hunslet Engine Co of Leeds. Between 1841 and 1935 the firm had built about 1,960 locomotives, making an average annual output of nearly 21 engines.

Peckett's managed to struggle through the Depression, but in the late forties the firm failed to change over to building diesels which most industrial users required, and by 1956, when Peckett's switched to this more economic power, its customers had gone elsewhere. The last steam engine to be built in Bristol was a tank engine for a Mozambique sugar estate. It was completed in June 1958. The very last locomotive left the works in February 1961 when the firm was taken over by the Reed Crane & Hoist Co Ltd. 2,166 engines had been built since 1864: an annual average output of just over 22.

Another factory concerned with railways was the Bristol Wagon & Carriage Works. In 1851 two more Quakers, John Fowler and Albert Fry, began making agricultural implements in Temple Street. When in 1856 Fowler left to establish his own firm in Leeds, Fry took his cousin Theodore into partnership. The latter left in 1866 and the Bristol Wagon Works was formed to take over the business with Albert Fry its managing director. A new factory was built at Lawrence Hill alongside the Midland Railway and connected by a siding. By 1875 the number of employees had reached 700. The firm had been renamed the Bristol Wagon & Carriage Works Co Ltd in 1869 as it built anything from wheelbarrows to railway carriages. Its main railway products were exported. Coach bodies for steam rail motors were built for the Great Northern, Great Western and Taff Vale railways, some of the power units being supplied by the Avonside Engine Co. In 1920 the firm was acquired by the Leeds Forge Co Ltd and in October 1923 this in turn was taken over by Cammell, Laird & Co which closed the Bristol works, causing 300 men to find alternative employment. The 13-acre site was bought in July 1924 by the Bristol Tramways & Carriage Company.

12. Named Trains

Most of the named trains using Temple Meads ran to and from Paddington. In 1849 a horse called 'Flying Dutchman' won both the Derby and the St Leger and so, not illogically, its name was transferred to the fastest train in the world, the 9.50am from Paddington which reached Bristol in 2½ hours conveying, until 1890, only first and second class passengers. During a period of financial constraints in 1867 the 'Flying Dutchman' was withdrawn for 18 months. It made its final broad gauge run on 20th May 1892 after which it became an undistinguished standard gauge train.

The original 'Cornishman', introduced in 1890, was the fastest train running between Paddington and Penzance. A broad gauge express, it carried third class passengers at a time when many important trains were only available to those with first or second class tickets. With the abolition from 1st October 1895 of the compulsory refreshment stop at Swindon, the 'Cornishman' made the first non-stop run to Bristol and did it at an average speed of 52.6 mph. During the summer months it ran in two parts and on 20th July 1896 the Newquay portion ran non-stop to Exeter avoiding Temple Meads station by using the Avoiding Line. In 1903 the 'Cornishman' was speeded to an average of 59.2 mph, cutting the Paddington to Bristol time to two hours for the first time. On 1st July 1904 the 'Cornish Riviera Limited' was introduced, running non-stop to Plymouth, and the 'Cornishman' was withdrawn.

Normally the 'Cornish Riviera Limited' avoided Bristol by travelling via Castle Cary. Here No 6004 *King George III* is seen leaving Temple Meads with the emergency Paddington to Penzance express in lieu of the 'Cornish Riviera', September/October 1939.
E J M Hayward

No 7019 *Fowey Castle* accelerates through Filton Junction with the Up 'Bristolian', 19th May 1959.

Hugh Ballantyne

No 5085 *Evesham Abbey* at Platform 9 Temple Meads with the last steam-hauled Up 'Bristolian', 12th June 1959. *Hugh Ballantyne*

The most famous train to the area was 'The Bristolian'. This was inaugurated in 1935 to mark the company's centenary and linked the cities in 105 minutes, 15 minutes faster than the previous best and requiring an average speed of 67 mph. Unusually the Down route differed from that of the Up. The Down 'Bristolian' travelled via Bath, but the Up went via Filton and Badminton. Although the latter route was three-quarters of a mile shorter, it involved climbing the 2¼ mile long Ashley Hill Bank at a gradient of 1 in 75, this more than cancelling out the shorter distance. Normally an engine of the 'Castle' class headed the seven-coach train. Withdrawn during WW2, the name was restored in 1951 and it was back on the 105 minute schedule in 1954. Probably the fastest run was by No 7018 *Drysllwyn Castle*, which in April 1958 ran from Bristol to Paddington in 93 minutes 50 seconds, giving an average speed of 75 mph, while a maximum speed of 102 mph was recorded. In the summer of 1959 the time was reduced to 100 minutes, this requiring an average speed of 71 mph, the first British postwar schedule to exceed 70 mph. By now steam had been ousted from this

prestigious train and haulage was by 'Warship' class diesel-hydraulic. The civil engineer, concerned at diesel-hydraulics exceeding 100 mph, imposed a limit of 90 mph, the 'Bristolian' timing necessarily being eased to 105 minutes. From 1961 onwards it is difficult to compare timings as loading was increased to 10 or 12 coaches and a stop at Bath added.

In 1951, the Festival of Britain year when wartime austerity was put in the past, 'The Merchant Venturer' was one of the new named trains introduced to brighten the railway scene. Leaving Paddington at 11.15am, it made a not very speedy run, calling at Bath Spa before arriving at Temple Meads at 1.22pm, finally terminating at Weston-super-Mare at 1.56pm. In the Up direction it was a semi-fast rather than a real express. It left Weston-super-Mare at 4.35pm and called at Yatton, Nailsea & Backwell, Temple Meads, Bath Spa, Chippenham, Swindon, and without stopping, slipped a coach at Reading General before arriving at Paddington at 8.00pm. Its average speed was 40 mph! The train's title was dropped in the 1965 timetable reorganisation.

Slip coach for Reading General at the rear of the Up 'Merchant Venturer', 11th September 1958. A composite coach, it carries first and third class passengers. In order that signalmen could check that a passing train had not accidentally detached a slip coach which would therefore be in danger of being struck by the next train, the last slip coach carried a red and white tail lamp instead of the normal red only. After the coach was slipped, should the slip guard require to sound a warning, a gong was provided – this can be seen below the right-hand and centre end windows. The photograph was taken passing Twerton Tunnel signalbox.

Author

'The Bristolian' was aimed at passengers wishing to travel from Paddington to Bristol in the morning and return in the late afternoon. To cater for those wishing to travel from Bristol to London, the 'Bristol Pullman' was inaugurated in 1960. Instead of being hauled by a locomotive, it had a power unit at each end of the train. A pushing power unit had been tried on stopping services, but was quite an innovation for an express, in fact it was a forerunner of today's HSTs. The train's livery was blue and white – quite a sight in an era when ordinary Pullmans were brown and white, and most ordinary coaches maroon. Although the 'Bristol Pullman' had some advantages such as air-conditioning, it rode roughly. It ran non-stop from Bristol to London via Badminton in 110 minutes, reaching the capital at 9.35am. Half an hour later it went back via Bath, reaching Bristol at noon. 30 minutes later it returned to Paddington in 115 minutes, making a final run of the day at 4.55pm from Paddington to Temple Meads via Badminton in 100 minutes. From the autumn it ran via Bath on the Up morning and Down evening trips, five minutes extra being allowed both ways. The 'Bristol Pullman' ceased running in 1973 when many ordinary coaches had air-conditioning, rode better than the 'Bristol Pullman' vehicles and did not charge a Pullman supplement.

Today the 'Night Riviera', conveying sleeping car passengers, leaves Paddington at five minutes to midnight and makes a fairly leisurely trip to Temple Meads arriving at 2.13am. It leaves 22 minutes later, arriving in Plymouth at 6.00am and Penzance at 8.24am allowing passengers plenty of time for a day's work or pleasure. 'The Brunel' is conveniently timed to leave Temple Meads at the not too early hour of 7.40am and arrives at Paddington 84 minutes later, having covered the 117¾ miles, including stops at Bristol Parkway and Swindon, at an average speed of 84 mph. 'The West Country Pullman' runs between Paddington and Temple Meads calling at Reading and Bath Spa, averaging 87 mph.

The Down 'Bristol Pullman' enters Bath Spa with the 5.40pm Paddington to Temple Meads, 13th June 1969.

PULLMAN DIESEL EXPRESS SERVICES
High-speed luxury travel

THE SOUTH WALES PULLMAN

THE BIRMINGHAM PULLMAN

and

THE BRISTOL PULLMAN

Mondays to Fridays only

Cover of Pullman Diesel leaflet, 1961

THE BRISTOL PULLMAN

MONDAYS TO FRIDAYS

BRISTOL TO LONDON

Bristol (Temple Meads)	dep.	8.15 a.m.	3.15 p.m.
Bath Spa	,,	8.32 a.m.	3.32 p.m.
Chippenham	,,	—	3.49 p.m.
London (Paddington)	arr.	10.10 a.m.	5.15 p.m.

LONDON TO BRISTOL

London (Paddington)	dep.	12.45 p.m.	5.45 p.m.
Chippenham	arr.	2. 9 p.m.	—
Bath Spa	,,	2.25 p.m.	7.20 p.m.
Bristol (Temple Meads)	,,	2.45 p.m.	7.40 p.m.

FARES

Between		First Class (Ordinary)		Second Class (Ordinary)		Supplementary Charges (Single journeys)	
		Single	Return	Single	Return	1st	2nd
		s. d.	s. d.	s. d.	s. d.	s. d.	s. d.
Bristol (Temple Meads)	Bath Spa	4 3	8 6	2 9	5 6	2 0	1 0
	Chippenham	8 6	17 0	5 9	11 6	2 6	1 0
	Paddington	41 0	82 0	27 6	55 0	10 0	5 0
Bath Spa	Chippenham	4 6	9 0	3 0	6 0	2 0	1 0
	Paddington	37 0	74 0	25 0	50 0	10 0	5 0
Chippenham	Paddington	33 0	66 0	22 0	44 0	10 0	5 0

NOTES APPLICABLE TO ALL PULLMAN DIESEL SERVICES.

1. Meals and refreshments served at every seat to the traditional high Pullman standards.
2. Limited accommodation, all seats reservable. Seats can be reserved in advance at stations and usual agencies for journeys from and to all calling points. Subsequent reservations may be effected with the Pullman Car Conductor on the train if accommodation is available.
3. Full supplementary charges payable for children.
4. Holders of Ordinary and Business Travel Season Tickets may travel by these trains on payment of the appropriate supplementary charge.
5. The fares and charges shown are liable to alteration.
6. Dogs, motor/scooters, perambulators, etc., are not conveyed on these services.

Bristol Pullman timings/fares, 1961

161

No 5061 *Sudeley Castle* (later re-named *Earl of Birkenhead*) at Temple Meads with a Down GWR express. 'The Devonian' coaches from the LMS would have been at the rear. Photograph taken c1937.

E J M Hayward

'The Devonian', 9.35am Bradford to Paignton near Yate, hauled by 'Jubilee' class No 45699 *Galatea*, 30th August 1959.

Hugh Ballantyne

The first of the north-east to south-west named expresses was 'The Devonian' and when originated in 1927 was rather a curiosity as, except during the summer, the majority of LMS coaches only ran from Bradford to Temple Meads, only three being handed over to the GWR to be worked to Torquay and Paignton. In 1939 'The Devonian' left Bradford at 10.25am and at Derby dropped a through coach to Bournemouth, while a Newcastle-upon-Tyne to Bristol coach was coupled on. The time of 4 hours 40 minutes for the hard 206 miles from Leeds to Bristol was excellent and the fastest of the day. At Temple Meads the through coaches were coupled to a Great Western express which, after quite a few stops, reached Torquay at 6.45pm and Paignton at 6.51, the 323 miles Bradford to Paignton taking 8 hours 26 minutes, giving an average speed of 38 mph. From May to September the whole train ran throughout

between Bradford and Kingswear. Withdrawn in 1939 it was reinstated in October 1946. Now an HST, it leaves Leeds at 7.59am, arrives at Temple Meads at 11.51 and Paignton at 1.41pm, averaging 54 mph.

In the summer of 1952 'The Cornishman' was introduced running from Wolverhampton through Birmingham, Cheltenham and Temple Meads to Plymouth and Penzance – a quite different train from that bearing the same name which ran 50 years earlier. 'The Cornishman' left Wolverhampton at 9.15am, reached Temple Meads at 12.28pm. It slipped a coach at Taunton and reached Penzance at 5.55pm. In the reverse direction it left Penzance at 10.30am, arrived in Temple Meads at 3.56pm and reached Wolverhampton at 7.28pm. In 1962 its route was changed to run from Cheltenham via the Lickey Incline, instead of Stratford-on-Avon, and

No D163 (later 46.026) *Leicestershire and Derbyshire Yeomanry* descending the gradient from Ashley Hill with 'The Cornishman', 8th May 1969.

Hugh Ballantyne

continued to Sheffield, later extended to Leeds and Bradford, though subsequently cut back to Leeds. In May 1973 it left Leeds at 7.41am, reaching Penzance at 4.37pm. In the spring of 1990, 'The Cornishman' is an HST and runs one of the longest distances in the country. It leaves Edinburgh at 7.25am, and taking the east coast route, reaches Temple Meads at 2.18pm and Penzance at 6.16pm.

The introduction of HSTs re-vitalised north-east to south-west services and other named trains were allocated to give them prestige and attract passengers. 'The Devon Scot' leaves Aberdeen at 8.55am and arrives in Plymouth at 9.05pm, while 'The Cornish Scot' leaves Edinburgh at 8.20am and, taking the west coast route, arrives in Temple Meads at 3.58pm and Penzance at 8.26pm. 'The Armada' runs between Leeds and Plymouth.

13. Three Perspectives of Working on the Railway in the Bristol Area

The Administration Side During the Late Thirties and Late Forties
by E J M Hayward

Following a boyhood enthusiasm for railways, my father made enquiries from an old school friend of his, Robert Hannington, the works Manager at Swindon, who suggested I saw the Divisional Superintendent at Bristol. Consequently I had an interview with the Superintendent's Chief Clerk and the Chief Staff Clerk in the Board Room of the former Bristol & Exeter Railway's offices. I was extremely fortunate for I was one of the first to be accepted following the economic cut-backs of the early 1930s. I joined the Great Western Railway Traffic Department in 1935, the company's centenary year. On 1st April I reported to the stationmaster at Keynsham & Somerdale on taking up my position as learner Junior Clerk.

My outstanding recollections of the time there were the lunch hours often spent in the West signalbox at the Bath end of the Down platform. Here I received encouragement in the signalman's art – passing bell signals and pulling

GREAT WESTERN RAILWAY.

R. G. POLE,
Divisional Superintendent.

Telegrams:
DIVISIONAL, G.W., BRISTOL STN.

Telephone:
21001 (PRIVATE BRANCH EXCHANGE).
EXTN. 59.

DIVISIONAL SUPERINTENDENT'S OFFICE,
TEMPLE MEADS STATION,
BRISTOL.

25th March, 1935.

Your reference:—

Please quote this reference:—

S1/-

Dear Sir,

With reference to your application for employment, I shall be glad to know if you will be prepared to report to the Station Master at Keynsham on Monday morning, April 1st to commence as a junior clerk learner.   Whilst learning your remuneration will be £25 per annum and when you are able to take up a turn of duty as junior clerk it will be increased to £45, the rate according to your age.

Yours truly,
for R.G.Pole.

Mr. E.J.M. Hayward,
   Monkton Coombe School,
      Bath.

EJM Hayward's letter of appointment as a junior clerk learner, 25th March 1935

165

Temple Meads: E J M Hayward, extreme right, standing on Platform 4 in 1938. No 5032 *Usk Castle* with unique Collett 8-wheel, 4000-gallon tender, has worked from Shrewsbury with the 10.32am Crewe to Plymouth and is awaiting the arrival of the 10.25am Bradford to Paignton, 'The Devonian', for forward working.

G H Soole/E J M Hayward Collection

levers – initially under supervision, but soon gaining assurance and competence. It was a modern and interesting box, opened less than two years previously.

It was responsible for a short section of less than half a mile to Keynsham East box in the Up, and to Fox's Wood box, 1½ miles in the Down direction. To reduce running time to the latter there were Intermediate Block signals. The Approach (1-2-1) bell code, used in both directions, was found only in short sections where the signalman needed advance warning of a train's approach. A track circuit buzzer was installed on the Down line and when it sounded, 'Train entering Section' (2 bells) was signalled to Fox's Wood. The hour's session usually included two expresses (4 bells) – the 11.15am Paddington to Weston-super-Mare and the 9.50am Ilfracombe (1.45pm Bristol) to Paddington – both receiving most careful attention. This practical experience greatly assisted my studies in the course 'Signalling and Safe Working' taken during the following winter, resulting in an examination pass – and later 'Merit'.

Another feature was the timing of passenger trains at close headway on the Down line from Keynsham around 5.30pm Monday to Fridays, at the time of clearing Fry's Somerdale workers homeward bound. Each timetable service varied slightly, but the sequence was: 5.24 to Bedminster and then onwards empty carriage stock (ECS) to Malago Vale; 5.30 (4.07 ex Swindon Jc) to Temple Meads and then ECS to Malago Vale; 5.35 to Filton Junction then ECS to Stoke Gifford for the engine to run round before stabling the coaches at Marsh Pond; 2.45 Paddington to Weston-super-Mare via Devizes passed through at 5.45. Empty stock for the 5.24 arrived in Keynsham at 4.00 from Malago Vale hauled by a 55XX class 2-6-2 tank engine and, after the locomotive had run round its train in the loops at the East box, crossed over the main lines and was stabled on Down Loop No 2. Stock for the 5.35 arrived at 4.37 from Marsh Pond hauled by a member of the 'Hall' class running tender-first. This was a longer train than that hauled by the 55XX and was stabled on Down Loop No 1.

After three months at Keynsham, I was transferred to the Passenger Train Section of the Divisional Superintendent's Office, Bristol. On summer Saturdays, to assist passenger train regulation west of the city, it was my pleasure to be on outside duty at Temple Meads westbound island platform Nos 3/5, to provide telephonic liaison regarding Down trains running to Parson Street Junction box, where on these occasions the District Chief Inspector was also present to advise on train regulation. Late and out-of-course running on these peak Saturdays, particularly from the North and Midlands, was quite normal. [A detailed account of the similar situation in the 1950s in Devon is given in David St John Thomas's *Summer Saturdays in the West* (David & Charles, 1973)].

In order to avoid excessive delays occurring between Parson Street Junction and Worle Junction, it was essential for the signalman at the former to be briefed with up-to-the-minute information regarding the running of Down express and local trains from Temple Meads. A local, stopping at Long Ashton, Flax Bourton,

Nailsea & Backwell, could delay a following express upwards of eight minutes before reaching Claverham loop to be overtaken. Similarly, Yatton was a bottleneck two-line station sandwiched between two pairs of running loops, followed by Puxton & Worle station before reaching Worle Junction and the Weston-super-Mare loop.

An off-season office investigation, in which I assisted, assessed from Guard's Train Reports the extent of delays suffered in this section of the line during the summer service, but WW2 intervened and no proposal for quadrupling was heard of subsequently – although doubtless the same situation recurred in the peak periods of the fifties.

The re-modelling and re-signalling of the Bristol area itself, with quadrupling between Filton Junction and Parson Street, had been completed by the time I joined the GWR. The track capacity then provided – by the Great Western four tracks from Bristol to Filton Junction and two tracks thence to Yate and by the LMS, two tracks from Bristol to Yate via Mangotsfield – contrasts with the two tracks available from Bristol to Yate at the present time

EJM Hayward's certificate for a satisfactory examination in the GWR's Rules and Regulations, 13th May 1936

and reflects the shorter running times with diesel traction, changed passenger and freight traffic flows with the closure of local stations and depots, and centralised MAS signalling. In the thirties, Great Western goods trains, (the term 'freight train' dates from the post-GWR era), were not scheduled to pass through Temple Meads, but travelled via the Avoiding Line and St Philip's Marsh. It involved 'crossings' at Bristol West, North Somerset Junction and Dr Day's Bridge Junction. LMS traffic routed via Bristol had to pass from, or to, West Depot via Temple Meads to avoid reversal, as in the case of No 14 Transfer to St Philip's in the early afternoon.

Despite being at the hub of the Great Western system, Bristol Temple Meads was shared with the LMS. The station master, responsible for operating functions, was designated 'Joint Superintendent' until the BR era, the appointment being made alternately from the two companies. Station commercial requirements normally covered by a stationmaster were dealt with by Passenger and Parcels Agents. In the late thirties, the Joint Superintendent was Amos Follows, an LMS appointment. A staunch 'Midlander' in every way, he maintained a certain independence and would challenge the Great Western Divisional Office when he disagreed with its instructions. Indeed, in some circumstances he seemed to lack proper respect for the Divisional Superintendent R G Pole for whom I held a deep awe, not lessened by the fact that his brother Felix had been the GWR's General Manager from 1921 to 1929. The Platform Inspectors, together with platform staff and shunters, were also joint staff, but there was also a Great Western Chief Inspector and staff with responsibility for guards and other matters inclusive of passenger train telegraphic advices. F W Coulam held this post in the thirties.

Following the outbreak of WW2, in December 1939 I joined the Royal Engineers and, after training at Longmoor, my service was mostly overseas in France, Persia, Iraq and Italy in Railway Operating Companies, Groups and Headquarters. Six and a half years later I resumed duty in the same Bristol office for seven months before starting a course of departmental training, followed by attachment to the Superintendent of the Line, Paddington, as a Passenger Train Runner (i.e. non-uniformed inspector) for a year. In 1949, following Nationalisation I joined the East African Railways & Harbours, part of the Colonial Service for 16 years, holding the post of District Traffic Superintendent in Kenya and Tanganyika/Tanzania.

The next contributor, Charlie Rust, was my colleague in the Divisional Office at Bristol. We worked for two summer seasons as part of a team of five in the excursion office planning travel and preparing advertising material. Charlie lived at 6 Lyncombe Hill, Bath, next door to John Allen, Stationmaster at Bath who lived in No 8 – a GWR house. As he lived less than 300 yds from the station, Charlie travelled home to lunch each day from Bristol leaving Temple Meads at noon on the 10.15 ex Taunton which arrived Bath 12.16. He returned on the 11.15 ex Paddington, leaving Bath at 1.00pm and arriving Temple Meads at 1.15.

A Stationmaster's Day at Bristol Temple Meads
by C R Rust, Stationmaster

(Reprinted from the *Railway Magazine*, September 1959, courtesy of the Editor)

Temple Meads station has 15 platforms and deals with 434 trains a day. Traffic is controlled by three signalboxes and there are three yards for storing and servicing empty coaches. In my position as Stationmaster, I am assisted by a staff of 636. Like most people in similar jobs, I try and keep to a routine in as many matters as possible, but in the operating department of a big railway there is always some problem cropping up which prevents one working according to plan.

I usually arrive at the station at 8.30am, or earlier on busy Saturdays, at holiday times, or when I have some important passengers to see off on one of the early trains. If I have not met the Chief Station Inspector on the way to my office, I contact him immediately and ascertain the up-to-date position. If things are normal and there is nothing needing my immediate attention, I spend the next 15 min. or so in the offices. Firstly, the soft hat and coat worn to the station is put away and the regulation bowler and dark grey overcoat is got out of the wardrobe and put ready. Then I look at my diary to see if there are any meetings to attend, important parties of persons to meet or see off, or staff to interview.

The morning mail and copies of the working notices and so on, which have arrived since the previous evening, are ready and waiting on my desk. I have a quick look through these and then go to the up main platform to see the 9 am express to Paddington. I shall meet the Chief Station Inspector and have a short talk with him, particularly in regard to the working until the completion of his turn of duty at 2pm. Then back to my office and for the next hour try and maintain the routine, for it is during this time that I see the inspectors in charge of the various sections of the staff under my control.

Firstly, there is the Ticket Inspector; in addition to any question regarding his staff, I discuss with him the arrangements for any special parties to be dealt with that day. Then follows the Guards' Inspector, who is responsible to me for the 201 guards at the station. I discuss with him any correspondence received that morning or other matters relating to guards or travelling ticket collectors. After the Guards' Inspector, the Yard Inspector arrives at about 9.30am. He has already visited at least two of the coaching depots and has been in touch with a third. Such questions as the position for coaches, siding accommodation, number of vehicles awaiting repairs and special coaches for parties are referred to. The last of the inspectors to be seen is the Carriage Servicing Inspector. He has 133 men to supervise and, apart from carriage cleaning matters, he frequently has a few staff problems on which he requires a ruling. After the departure of the Carriage Servicing Inspector I have a short talk with my Chief Clerk, usually on staff matters.

My activities after 10 am have to be 'built around' the important requirements of each particular day, as indeed on most days, I proceed to the down main-line platform to meet the 8.45am from Paddington – the down 'Bristolian' – due at 10.25am, calling on my way to look at a waiting room or toilet. I have met off the 'Bristolian' in recent months Ambassadors to the Court of St. James, High Commissioners, members of the Government, bankers, industrialists, and parties from the Commonwealth. Usually I get to know from some source or another when important persons or parties are travelling and have arranged beforehand by what exit they will leave the station and that the cars or coaches meeting them are suitable positioned and the police advised. The compliments which I have had paid to this famous Western Region express are many and I always get a great deal of satisfaction (not to mention relief on some occasions) when the train runs in punctually or, quite often, a few minutes early.

Now I return to my offices to deal with the correspondence and do some clerical work. On this 'typical day' the clerical work may involve arranging the platforms for a heavy programme of excursion and relief trains at the weekend. In an endeavour to see that the public are given correct information, all the members of the platform staff are supplied with duplicated notices giving particulars of special trains, the platforms at which they are to be dealt with and any alterations to the standard platform arrangements necessitated by the additional trains. Although today it may be platforming of extra trains, tomorrow it may be plans to examine in regard to modernisation or proposed new working to consider.

On this day the working is favourable and I am

WORKING OF PASSENGER GUARDS

WEEK-DAYS.

BRISTOL.

No. of Turn and Guard's Name.	Booked Time. On duty.	Booked Time. Off duty.	Train.	From	To	Time due.	Gross working hours.	Remarks.
Bruford No. 1.	a.m. 5 45	p.m. 2 5	a.m. 6 20	Bristol	Plymouth (North Road)	a.m. 10 2	h. m.	Head to Tiverton Junc., sole to Plymouth.
				Walk to Mutley.				
			10 34	Mutley	Bristol	p.m. 1 58	8 20	Junior.
Lock No. 2.	a.m. 9 25	p.m. 6 10	a.m. 9 40	Bristol	Paddington ..	p. m. 12 40		Head.
			p.m. 2 45	Paddington ..	Bristol	5 55	8 45	Head to Newbury thence sole.
Matthews No. 4.	p.m. 12 15	p.m. 7 45	p.m. 1 0	Bristol	Salisbury ..	p.m. 3 20		Head Trowbridge to Westbury, otherwise Sole.
				Assist as required at Salisbury.				
			4 42	Salisbury ..	Bristol	7 15	7 30	
Bundy No. 5.	p.m. 5 30	a.m. 1 15	p.m. 6 0	Bristol	Paddington ..	p.m. 8 50		Sole to Swindon, thence Head.
			10 0	Paddington ..	Bristol	a.m. 1 2	7 45	Tail guard.
Brooks No. 7.	noon 12 0	p.m. 9 0	p.m. 12 10	Bristol	Paddington ..	p.m. 2 25		{ Sole **M.O.** { Junior **M.X.**
			p.m. 5 15	Paddington ..	Bristol	8 43	9 0	Head to Reading. Sole beyond.

Page from GWR 'Programme of Working of Passenger Guards, 1st February 1919' able to get back to the platform again for the 11.45am express to London, the down 'Cornishman' and the up 'Devonian'. I discuss with the Chief Station Inspector a connectional problem which has arisen. The question of connections is an ever-present one at Bristol because of its geographical position and often my inspectors and I have to meet the wrath of an angry passenger who has missed his (or her) connection and cannot understand why we did not keep a train with 300 passengers waiting.

After a break for lunch I pay a visit to East Box, where there are 368 levers. Three special-class signalmen are on duty continuously, not to mention the 'booking boy' who has to make full train register entries for 24 block instruments and bells. I am always sorry that my busy days do not permit me to spend more time in the signalboxes. On from the East Box, I go to Dr. Day's Carriage Sidings, a coaching depot with 20 roads including a new 'fuelling and inspection road' for diesel multiple-units. This depot is some half-mile from the station.

West Box was visited yesterday and one day during the week I must go to Malago Vale Sidings, about 1½ miles on the west side of the station, and also visit Lawrence Hill Junction Sidings – three-quarters of a mile from the station on the former LMR line and where the stock for the Bradford, York and Newcastle trains is stabled.

I make a call at the Chief Inspector's office to see the man on duty at 2pm and at 2.30pm the Yard Inspector brings me a shunter who was responsible for a derailment a few weeks ago. He has a good record and an admonishment meets the case.

Now there is another hour's clerical work, of which there is an abundance these days, and after signing what letters have been typed, back to the platforms for the important evening trains. The up 'Bristolian' – 4.30 Bristol to Paddington must be seen away, but the working of other important cross-country trains and the comfort of passengers in them is not overlooked.

I return to my office shortly after 5pm, sign the remainder of my letters and have a short talk with my Chief Clerk on the events of the day. I glance at the diary to see what is in store for the following day, and at 5.45pm the bowler hat is returned to its peg, and the soft hat and light coat got out and then home to what I hope will be a quiet night. I am, however, 'on call' continuously, and in the event of a derailment in my area, or an emergency likely to seriously affect the working at Bristol, I have to turn out at once. The winter weather also brings problems and I am always apprehensive when snow is forecast at night. The electrical equipment at the East and West Signalboxes are quickly affected and a snowfall at night always brings me hurrying back on duty whatever the hour.

I have made no mention of telephone calls which in modern business are of necessity numerous and I get my share. Although I have referred to a few trains only, I endeavour to see all the important trains as frequently as circumstances permit and vary my day's work in order to do this.

There are such things as interviews with staff who have some personal problems, discussions with the staff representatives of two local departmental committees, special inspections of various parts of the station accommodation, and meeting with members of the public in regard to some special arrangements, or with representatives of the 100 cabmen who ply for hire at the station. All these things have to be fitted in and go to make up a day in the life of the Stationmaster at Bristol.

I sometimes wonder how much my day differed from that of my predecessors or what the Stationmaster's day at Bristol will be like in twenty years' time. My guess is that past, present and future will not be greatly different, and call to mind a Superintendent under whom I served for some years [R G Pole, Bristol Divisional Superintendent], who used to say 'There is nothing new in railways'. While this is no doubt rather too sweeping a statement, I can recollect many times when I thought I had the answer to a particular problem, only to be told 'That was tried thirty years ago but did not work because of . . .'

Memories of North Somerset Junction and Doctor Day's Bridge Junction Signalboxes, 1957–1959 by Dr A J G Dickens

I was fortunate enough to have a vacation job for three years with BR(WR) as a Special Class Telegraphist, spending the summers of 1957 and 1958 at North Somerset Junction signalbox, and that of 1959 at Dr Day's Bridge Junction signalbox. I was over 18 years old and so could work on the night shift from 10pm to 6am, which I did for 18 consecutive weeks including all my scheduled rest days. I was the 'booking boy', dealing with all Train Register entries and telephone messages. Each signalbox had approximately ten telephones covering a different operating or route circuit. In practice, I was also allowed, on occasion and under supervision, to pull and return the point and signal levers in the two, long manual frames; 93 levers in North Somerset Junction and 112 in Dr Day's. I have many happy memories of these great summers, and especially of actually being a part of the 'Great Western' itself.

The steam highlight of my night-duties was undoubtedly watching No 3440 *City of Truro* storming past North Somerset Junction around 12.40am on the Up Main towards Bath. She hauled the 4.45pm Plymouth to Paddington parcels train, sometimes with more than 20 vans. This working preceded the Penzance to Paddington Up Royal Mail which left Temple Meads at 12.55am. The parcels train left Temple Meads at 12.35am and had to reach Bath without delaying the Up Mail which was steadily gaining on it. Explanations to Bristol Control about delays to the Mail were best avoided by giving a clear run to *City of Truro*. Both of the two night-duty signalmen and myself were always at the windows to watch her appear round the curve from Temple Meads East signalbox, pass Kingsland Road sidings, our signalbox and then disappear between East Depot Up and Down yards towards St Anne's Park with a long train of vans behind her. The up Mail was headed by a 'King', or more usually, a 'Castle' and was the subject of special attention by Control regarding time-keeping – a fact only too well-known to us.

The priority at North Somerset Junction was always to avoid delaying trains on the main Temple Meads to Bath line. The art lay in the timing of trains to and from South Wales and the North of England round the relief loop from Dr Day's, across the main line and round the Bristol Avoiding Line via St Philip's Marsh. The 'regulation' of freight trains was usually involved, with crews quite often changing on the loop and with a 'Dispatcher' based in a trackside office who would advise me when a train was ready to move on. 'Regulation' meant checking the whereabouts of any higher-class train on the main line which might be delayed while the one on the loop started, slowly crossed the main and then rounded the speed-restricted curves to Marsh Junction signalbox en route to St Philip's Marsh. Such checks on time margins might include telephoning to Fox's Wood, Keynsham East, Bath Station, or even Bathampton signalboxes, as well as to Temple Meads East signalbox. On Friday nights there would be between 6 and 14 Wakes Week passenger specials from the north to Devon and Cornwall, all stopping on the loop for crew changes or main line 'margin' reasons. On a hot August night all the coach windows would be down on the train coming to a stand – but these would be quickly slammed shut as the familiar, but pungent, smell from the knacker's yard next to North Somerset Junction signalbox wafted remorselessly across the lines! On a wet or humid night the effect could be truly dramatic. These trains would usually all be on their way before the Up 'Waker', the Penzance to Paddington Night Sleeper which left Temple Meads at 3.55am and was another train not to be delayed by us.

My last summer as a Special Class Telegraphist was at Dr Day's, and at first it seemed strange to be at the other end of the loop lines from North Somerset Junction – of course we used to blame my former colleagues for always delaying 'our' South Wales trains because of 'their' London ones. The volume of freight traffic was then high, and freight trains after passing Dr Day's and Lawrence Hill would commonly need banking assistance from Stapleton Road to Filton Junction. Very careful signalbox liaison was needed over train running margins because a maximum length, 60-wagon train, stopped at our Home Signal at Dr Day's, would still have its guard's van the Marsh Junction side of the main London line at North Somerset Junction, so bringing everything around to an unscheduled halt.

As can be seen, I still have many happy memories of those three summers during which the need for true team-work in good railway operating was always being brought home to me. It would simply not be the same to work nowadays in the truly omnipotent Power Box at Temple Meads!

TAUNTON, MINEHEAD, EXETER, DAWLISH, TEIGNMOUTH, NEWTON ABBOT, TORQUAY, PAIGNTON and PLYMOUTH

TO	**RETURN FARES, SECOND CLASS, From**					
	Bath Spa	Avonmouth Dock Shire-hampton Sea Mills	Bristol (T.M.)	Clifton Down Redland Mont-pelier	Filton Junc-tion	Stapleton Road Lawrence Hill
	s. d.	s. d.	s. d.	s. d.	s. d.	s. d.
TAUNTON	13/6	12/6	11/0	12/0	12/6	11/6
MINEHEAD	18/0	17/0	15/6	16/6	17/0	16/0
EXETER (St. David's)	20/6	19/6	18/0	19/0	19/6	18/6
DAWLISH	22/6	21/6	20/0	21/0	21/6	20/6
TEIGNMOUTH	23/0	22/0	20/6	21/6	22/0	21/0
NEWTON ABBOT	24/0	23/0	21/6	22/6	23/0	22/0
TORQUAY	25/0	24/0	22/6	23/6	24/0	23/0
PAIGNTON	25/0	24/0	22/6	23/6	24/0	23/0
PLYMOUTH	32/6	31/6	30/0	31/0	31/6	30/6

DAILY
TAUNTON
s. d.

RETURN FARE 11 / 0 SECOND CLASS
from BRISTOL (Temple Meads)
FORWARD AND RETURN BY ANY TRAIN THE SAME DAY

SUNDAYS
EXETER

FROM	DEPART		RETURN FARE SECOND CLASS
	a.m.	a.m.	s. d.
BRISTOL—			
TEMPLE MEADS	7 0	11a 40	**18/0**
		p.m.	
EXETER (St. David's) ... arr.	9 35	2 0	a—Change at Taunton.

Return by any train the same day affording a service through to destination.

Day Return fares, September 1963

SPECIAL CHEAP DAY RETURN FARES

Available any day by any train after 9.30 a.m.

(Where First Class accommodation is available, First Class Tickets are issued at approximately 50% above the Third Class fare.)

All fares are Third Class, in shillings (s.) and pence (d.)

From ASHLEY HILL
- to Bath Spa ... 2
- Clevedon ... 2 9
- Henbury ... 2 2
- Oldfield Park ... 1 2
- Severn Beach ... 2 8
- Weston-super-Mare 3 3

From ASHTON GATE
- to Portishead ... 1 7*

From AVONMOUTH DOCK
- to Bristol (T.M.) ... 1 6
- Clevedon ... 3 3
- Clifton Down ... 1 0
- Lawrence Hill ... 1 5
- Redland ... 0 7
- Sea Mills ... 0 5
- Stapleton Road ...
- Weston-super-Mare 3 5

From BATH SPA
- to Bristol (T.M.) ... 1 10
- Clevedon ... 3 9
- Keynsham & S. ... 0 4
- Portishead ... 4 8
- St. Anne's Park ... 3 9
- Severn Beach ... 4 3
- Weston-super-Mare 4 3

From BEDMINSTER
- to Bath Spa ... 2 0
- Clevedon ... 2 3
- Ham Green Halt. ... 1 4*
- Oldfield Park ... 1 11*
- Pill ... 1 7*
- Portbury ... 2 3*
- Portishead ... 3 0
- Weston-super-Mare 3 2
- Yatton ... 2 2

From BRISLINGTON
- to Clevedon ... 2 6
- Weston-super-Mare 3 3

From BRISTOL (T.M.)
- to Avonmouth Dock ... 1 6
- Clevedon ... 3 3
- Ham Green Halt. ... 1 4*
- Henbury ... 1 5

From BRISTOL (T.M.) *continued*
- to Keynsham & S. ... 0 10
- Oldfield Park ... 1 9
- Pill ... 1 5*
- Portbury ... 1 8*
- Portishead ... 1 10*
- St. Andrew's Road ... 1 7
- Salford ...
- Sea Mills ... 1 2
- Severn Beach ... 2 4
- Shirehampton ... 1 3
- Weston-super-Mare 3 4
- Yatton ... 2 1

From CLEVEDON
- to Bristol (T.M.) ... 3 3
- Weston-super-Mare 1 9

From CLIFTON BRIDGE
- to Portishead ... 1 7*

From CLIFTON DOWN
- to Avonmouth Dock ... 1 0
- Clevedon ... 4
- Oldfield Park ... 2 2
- Portishead ... 2 8
- St. Andrew's Road ... 3
- Severn Beach ... 2 0
- Weston-super-Mare 3 3

From FILTON JUNC.
- to Bath Spa ... 2 4
- Clevedon ... 3 10
- Oldfield Park ... 2 3
- Severn Beach ... 2 6
- Weston-super-Mare 3 3

From FLAX BOURTON
- to Clevedon ... 1 8
- Weston-super-Mare 2 4

From HAM GREEN HALT
- to Bedminster ... 1 4*
- Bristol (T.M.) ... 1 4*
- Parson Street ... 1 5

From HENBURY
- to Ashley Hill ... 2
- Bath Spa ... 2 8
- Bristol (T.M.) ... 1 5
- Clevedon ... 3 0
- Horfield ... 1 4
- Lawrence Hill ... 2
- Oldfield Park ... 2 8
- Severn Beach ... 1 4
- Stapleton Road ... 1
- Weston-super-Mare 4 -

From HORFIELD
- to Bath Spa ... 2 3
- Clevedon ... 3 0
- Henbury ... 1 2
- Oldfield Park ... 2 1
- Severn Beach ... 1 7
- Weston-super-Mare 3 3

From KEYNSHAM & S.
- to Bath Spa ... 0 4
- Bristol (T.M.) ... 0 10
- Clevedon ... 3 3
- Oldfield Park ... 2 2
- Weston-super-Mare 4 3

From LAWRENCE HILL
- to Avonmouth Dock ... 1 5
- Bath Spa ... 2 0
- Clevedon ... 2 5
- Ham Green Halt ... 1 7*
- Henbury ... 2 -
- Oldfield Park ... 1 4
- Pill ... 1 7*
- Portishead ... 2 0*
- St. Andrew's Road ... 2 0
- Severn Beach ... 2 2
- Shirehampton ... 2 0
- Weston-super-Mare 3 2
- Yatton ... 2 6

From MONTPELIER
- to Avonmouth Dock ... 1 1
- Clevedon ... 2 8
- Oldfield Park ... 2 2
- Portishead ... 2 6*
- St. Andrew's Road ... 1 4

From MONTPELIER *continued*
- to Sea Mills ... 0 8
- Severn Beach ... 1 9
- Shirehampton ... 1 0
- Weston-super-Mare 3 3

From NAILSEA
- to Clevedon ... 1 5
- Weston-super-Mare 2 -

From NORTH FILTON
- to Severn Beach ... 1 6
- Weston-super-Mare 3 9

From OLDFIELD PARK
- to Bristol (T.M.) ... 1 9
- Clevedon ... 2
- Keynsham & S. ... 2 2
- Portishead ... 4
- Severn Beach ... 7
- St. Anne's Park ... 3
- Weston-super-Mare 4 3

From PARSON STREET
- to Bath Spa ... 2 1
- Clevedon ... 2 -
- Ham Green Halt ... 1 2*
- Oldfield Park ... 2 0
- Pill ... 2 -
- Portbury ...
- Portishead ... 2 2*
- Severn Beach ... 2 4
- Weston-super-Mare 3 -

From PILL
- to Bedminster ... 4*
- Bristol (T.M.) ... 5*
- Parson Street ... 2*

From PORTBURY
- to Bedminster ... 7*
- Bristol (T.M.) ... 8*
- Parson Street ... 5*

From PORTISHEAD
- to Ashton Gate ... 1 -
- Bedminster ... 2 8
- Bristol (T.M.) ... 9*
- Clifton Bridge ... 10*
- Parson Street ... 8*

From PUXTON & WORLE
- to Bristol (T.M.) ... 3 0
- Clevedon ... 5

From REDLAND
- to Avonmouth Dock ... 1 0
- Bath Spa ... 2 2
- Clevedon ... 2 8
- Oldfield Park ... 2 2
- Portishead ... 2 6*
- St. Andrew's Road ... 7*
- Sea Mills ... 0 7
- Severn Beach ... 0
- Shirehampton ... 3
- Weston-super-Mare 3 3

From ST. ANDREW'S ROAD
- to Bristol (T.M.) ... 1 7
- Clevedon ... 3
- Lawrence Hill ... 6*
- Montpelier ... 4
- Redland ... 7*
- Sea Mills ... 10
- Stapleton Road ... 9
- Weston-super-Mare 3

From ST. ANNE'S PARK
- to Bath Spa ... 5*
- Clevedon ... 2 7
- Oldfield Park ... 2 7
- Portishead ... 3*
- Weston-super-Mare 3 3

From SALTFORD
- to Bristol (T.M.) ... 1 4
- Weston-super-Mare 4 3

From SEA MILLS
- to Bristol (T.M.) ... 1 2
- Clevedon ... 3 0
- Clifton Down ... 6
- Montpelier ... 0 8
- Redland ... 0 7
- Severn Beach ... 5
- Weston-super-Mare 3 6

From SEVERN BEACH
- to Bristol (T.M.) ... 2 4
- Clifton Down ... 1 8
- Lawrence Hill ... 2 2
- Montpelier ... 9
- Redland ... 9
- Stapleton Road ... 1 10

From SHIREHAMPTON
- to Bristol (T.M.) ... 3
- Clevedon ... 0 10
- Clifton Down ... 0
- Lawrence Hill ... 7*
- Montpelier ... 0
- Redland ... 0
- Stapleton Road ... 1
- Weston-super-Mare 3 6

From STAPLETON RD.
- to Avonmouth Dock ... 5
- Bath Spa ... 2 7*
- Clevedon ... 4
- Ham Green Halt ... 4
- Henbury ... 4
- Oldfield Park ... 8*
- Pill ... 2 -*
- Portishead ...
- St. Andrew's Road ... 9
- Severn Beach ... 1 10
- Shirehampton ... 3
- Weston-super-Mare 2 6
- Yatton ...

From WESTON MILTON HALT
- to Bristol (T.M.) ... 3 3
- Clevedon ... 1 8

From WESTON-SUPER-MARE
- to Bath Spa ... 4 3
- Clevedon ... 3 9

From YATTON
- to Bristol (T.M.) ... 2 2
- Weston-super-Mare 1 6

* Available by any train throughout the day.

Cheap Day Return Fares table. summer 1955

174

Bibliography

Allen, C J, *Titled Trains of the Western* (Ian Allan, 1974)

Clinker, C R, *Closed Stations & Goods Depots* (Avon Anglia, 1978)

Clinker, C R, 'Railway Development at Bristol', *Railway Magazine* (September, October, November 1956)

Cocks, R H, 'Notable Railway Stations: Temple Meads', *Railway Magazine* (October 1900)

Cooke, R A, *Track Layout Diagrams of the GWR and BR WR.* Section 16, 1974; Section 19, 1975; Section 20, 1988; Section 21, 1988 (R A Cooke)

Cornock, W, 'Railway Warehouses and Goods Depots', *Railway & Travel Monthly* (June 1914)

Cullen, E, 'Industrial Development by Railways: Canon's Marsh Extension', *Great Western Railway Magazine* (June 1906)

Fellows, Canon R B, 'Rival Routes to Bristol', *Railway World* (November/December 1960)

Hateley, R, *Industrial Locomotives of South Western England* (Industrial Railway Society, 1977)

Hawkins, C & Reeve, G, *LMS Engine Sheds, Volume 2* (Wild Swan, 1981)

Leleux, S A, *Brotherhoods, Engineers* (David & Charles, 1965)

Lyons, E, *An Historical Survey of Great Western Engine Sheds, 1947* (Oxford Publishing Company, 1972)

Lyons, E & Mountford, E, *An Historical Survey of Great Western Engine Sheds, 1837–1947* (Oxford Publishing Company, 1979)

MacDermot, E T, Clinker, C R & Nock, O S, *History of the Great Western Railway* (Ian Allan, 1964/7)

Maggs, C G, *Bristol & Gloucester Railway* (Oakwood Press, 1969)

Maggs, C G, *Bristol Port Railway & Pier* (Oakwood Press, 1975)

Maggs, C G, *Rail Centres: Bristol* (Ian Allan, 1989)

Maggs, C G, 'Railways between Bristol and Bath', *Railway World* (February, March, April 1960)

Nock, O S, 'Resorts for Railfans, Bristol', *Trains Illustrated* (May 1952)

Norris, J, *The Bristol & South Wales Union Railway* (Railway & Canal Historical Society, 1985)

Oakley, M, *Railways in Avon* (Avon County Planning Department, 1983)

Oakley, M, *Railways in Avon* (Avon Anglia, 1986)

Oakley, M, *Railway Stations & Halts in Avon, A Photographic Record* (Avon County Council, 1984)

Pell-Hiley, A G, 'Twenty Four Hours at Bristol', *Railway Magazine* (October 1909)

Popplewell, L, *A Gazetteer of the Railway Contractors and Engineers of the West Country 1830–1914* (Melledgen Press, 1983)

Railway Correspondence & Travel Society, *Locomotives of the Great Western Railway* (RCTS, 1952–74)

Robertson, K & Abbott, D, *GWR The Badminton Line* (Alan Sutton, 1988)

Vaughan, A, *A Pictorial Record of Great Western Architecture* (Oxford Publishing Company, 1977)

Vincent, M, *Lines to Avonmouth* (Oxford Publishing Company, 1979)

Vincent, M, *Reflections on the Portishead Branch* (Oxford Publishing Company, 1983)

Warnock, D W, *The Bristol & North Somerset Railway 1863–1884* (Avon Anglia, 1978)

Warnock, D W & Parsons, R G, *The Bristol & North Somerset Railway Since 1884* (Avon Anglia, 1979)

Whitley, H S, 'The Canon's Marsh Extension, Bristol', *Great Western Railway Magazine* (July 1906)

Wray, A, 'Brave Jack Chiddy', *Avon Valley Railway 1990 Year Book* (Avon Valley Railway, 1990)

Acknowledgement

Grateful acknowledgement is due to Norman Slipp for checking the manuscript.

Westerleigh sidings, looking north, 21st April 1960.   *Author*